T0001599

It can be a crushing burden thinking that all depends upon me. Thomas Davis helps pours encouragement into us by the bucketful. Rooted in rich theology, clothed in contemporary language and peppered with helpful illustrations, it is a transfusion for anaemic faith, a shot in the arm for us all as we seek to take seriously our Saviour's commission to be His witnesses. The study questions at the close of each chapter drive home the truths just taught. We are left concluding, 'Anyone can do it!'

MIKE MELLOR
Evangelist and writer

Just hearing the word 'evangelism' induces guilt for many Christians. None of us are the evangelists we desire to be; and who needs to be reminded of that yet again? That is why this book by Thomas Davis is welcomed. Here is an uplifting and encouraging primer on evangelism. Davis undergirds the disciple of Christ with sound theology, practical help, and a refreshing outlook. It takes away the fear of evangelism by centring it upon the greatness of God, the grace of Christ, and the work of the Holy Spirit through each of us as unique individuals. I would love to put this book in every Christian's hands.

JASON HELOPOULOS
Senior Pastor at University Reformed Church, East Lansing, MI.

I have been waiting years for this book! It proves that strong meat can be easily digested and beautifully presented. Winsome evangelism requires robust content and an enthusiastic messenger, and this book will both inform and motivate. The passion of the author is infectious. Well-illustrated and applied with powerful relevance it makes for a compulsive read. Value will be added if a church or group of friends read it together, thoughtfully and prayerfully chewing through the issues. If you have a sense that you just can't witness, then you have just grasped the first principle of this book. God is powerful and He delights to empower the weak.

DAVID C. MEREDITH
Mission Director, Free Church of Scotland

This is a wonderfully encouraging and compelling book on evangelism. With a pastor's heart and a passion for theology, Thomas reminds us of how incredible God is, how brilliant His plans are, how good the gospel is, and how blessed we are to share it. I highly recommend it.

ANDY LONGWE
Minister of London City Presbyterian Church

THOMAS
DAVIS

GOD
IS
GOD
&
YOU
ARE
YOU

*Finding
Confidence For
Sharing Our Faith*

CHRISTIAN
FOCUS

Copyright © Thomas Davis 2023

paperback ISBN 978-1-5271-0938-4
e-book ISBN 978-1-5271-0997-1

10 9 8 7 6 5 4 3 2 1

Published in 2023
by
Christian Focus Publications Ltd,
Geanies House, Fearn, Ross-shire,
IV20 1TW, Great Britain.

www.christianfocus.com

Cover design by Tom Barnard

Printed by Bell and Bain, Glasgow

MIX
Paper | Supporting
responsible forestry
FSC
www.fsc.org
FSC® C007785

Contents

Dedicated to my parents, Neil and Kinny Davis,
who have given me continual support,
encouragement and love throughout my life,
and for whom I am so thankful to God.

Introduction:
God is God and You are You

This is a book about evangelism. Evangelism is crucial: it is urgent; it is exciting; it is wonderful. There is nothing more thrilling than to see God at work in people's lives and to see men, women, boys and girls discovering the incredible joy and peace that come from knowing Jesus. Evangelism is such an essential and amazing part of being a Christian.

But it is also hard. Really hard. And for me, and for nearly every Christian I have ever met, sharing our faith with other people is the area of our Christian lives where we feel at our most useless.

And this can be so frustrating. It is frustrating because we know that we *need* to do it. All around us there are people who desperately need to hear the gospel, who desperately need to find the salvation and healing that only Jesus can give.

It is also frustrating because we also know that we *want* to do it. We long to see people come to faith, we pray for the opportunities to talk about Jesus, we want God to use us in any way He can to help someone come to faith in Jesus.

When it comes to evangelism, we know we need to do it and we know that we want to do it. But so often, both of these convictions are crushed by the overwhelming feeling that I just *can't* do it. If that is how you feel, then this book is written for you. This book is written to tell you that, when it comes to sharing your faith, you absolutely *can* do it.

We need to hear that because most of the time we feel the opposite. When it comes to evangelism, we can feel nervous, guilty, inadequate, sometimes even paralysed. Because of that, we often give up before we even try. Faced with that reality, it can be very helpful to learn more skills for how to share our faith. And there are lots of superb books that can help teach you the *how* of evangelism.[1] But learning more about how to share our faith is not the only way of overcoming the 'I can't do it' feelings. There is something else we can do, something that can make a massive difference. We can look at the Bible and discover that, within God's Word, there is a wealth of theological truth that is a powerhouse of encouragement for evangelism. Skills are important, experience is invaluable, but the key to recognising that you really can share your faith is to learn that as you step out to share the gospel, there is a tidal wave of incredible theology backing you up every step of the way. And at the heart of that theology lie two truths that we must never forget.

The first is that *God is God*. One of the reasons why sharing our faith is hard is because, for many people today, God seems weak, old-fashioned and irrelevant – and that's if He even exists at all. But none of that is true. God is not weak, not old-fashioned, not irrelevant and most definitely not non-existent. God is God! He is today what He has always been and always will be; the infinite, eternal and unchangeable Absolute of all reality, the all-powerful God who is calling us all to faith in His Son, Jesus Christ. And, as this book will go on to explore, even the tiniest step that you take to share the good news of Jesus Christ is done in the strength and service of the God who actually *is* God.

---

1. Three that I have found hugely helpful are *Out of the Saltshaker and Into the World* by Rebecca Manley Pippert, *Honest Evangelism* by Rico Tice, and *Know and Tell the Gospel* by John Chapman. See bibliography on page 145 for more details.

The second key truth is that *You are You*. Often, our evangelism is also crippled by the feeling that a good evangelist is someone who is everything that you are not. We see our weaknesses, our insecurities, our lack of eloquence, knowledge and confidence, and we conclude that if there's a good evangelist in the room, it definitely isn't me. And if that's true, then we conclude that to share our faith we need to become someone else. But the thing is, it is not true. It is completely untrue. You don't need to be someone that you aren't. God has not called a select group of elite Christians to tell the world about Jesus. He has called all of us to make disciples of all nations. And within that, He has made you, you. You are you, and that is exactly who God can use to tell people about Jesus. When it comes to sharing your faith, you must never, ever forget that God is God and you are you.

Alongside these, the following pages will explore some other key theological truths that empower evangelism. The book is in two parts, the first focuses on the fact that God is God, the second that you are you. Each chapter also contains study questions that I hope will help you think about each chapter topic a little more.

I want to close this introduction by saying that this book is not giving you the reflections of an expert evangelist. I have been a Christian for over twenty-five years, I have been a pastor for the past eight, and of all the areas of my life as a follower of Jesus, I think sharing my faith is the area I feel the least good at and the most frustrated about. That means that I have not written this book because of what I *have*. I have written it because of what I *need*. And I hope that, in reading this book, you will discover what I have discovered, that the key to evangelism is not super-confidence or elite skill. The key is to rest more and more on the incredible theology that God has revealed in Scripture.

At the heart of that theology is the amazing truth that God is God and you are you.

PART ONE
GOD IS GOD

Chapter One

God is God

∞∞∞

Sharing your faith is something that nearly every Christian finds very difficult. If you feel like you are terrible at it then I know how you feel, and you know how I feel. Jesus said that the harvest is plentiful but the labourers are few. Often, we feel like adding that the labourers are also awful at their job and, most of the time, feel a bit terrified. Because of that, we often just give up, resigning ourselves to having to live with feelings of guilt and failure. Or, sometimes we try to get better at it. To do that, we try to learn how we can improve. And that's a great thing to do: learning how to start conversations, how to listen well, how to build up relationships, all these things are crucial. These are skills that need to be taught and developed in all our local churches and they can be very helpful. But before learning all of that, there is an even bigger lesson we need to learn, or maybe re-learn. When it comes to sharing our faith, the single most important thing we need to know is that God is God.

God is God. That is the foundational truth of all Christian theology. When we say God is 'something', what we are trying to do is describe the nature of God. But that is not easy, because God is in a category all of His own. Nothing else has His nature, nothing else is in that category. That is why, when we talk about what God is, we need to use our biggest language. Immutable. Immense. Eternal. Incomprehensible. These are the kind of words we need. He is almighty; He is most wise, most holy, most free, most absolute. He is as big and as glorious and as majestic and as loving as it is possible to be. That's why it takes the entire universe to declare His glory. That's why learning about Him never gets boring. That's why He is worthy of our worship forever. The foundational truth of all Christian theology is that God is God.

But it is also the foundational truth of all Christian evangelism. And the reason we need to learn, or re-learn this is because, at the heart of our feelings of fear and inadequacy about sharing our faith, lies a set of relentless niggles telling us that God is a whole lot of other things. So **we can think that God is weak**, like a politician that hardly anyone wants to vote for, or a high street shop that is in the slow, painful process of going out of business. If you look at the population of whatever country you live in, the chances are it looks like Christianity is losing the battle for numbers, and the task of evangelism looks near impossible. And if you pick a friend or family member, even one single person can seem like a monumental task. How are they going to change? How can you get them to listen? How can you even bring God into the conversation at all? The hurdles look huge, and at that moment it's all too easy for our evangelistic fire to be quenched by a flood of niggles telling us that God is weak.

Or **we can think that God is distant**. So maybe in generations gone by, He would show Himself and do amazing things, but days like those are history. It's easy to think that Christians were much better then anyway, so no wonder God isn't very interested now. And even if we do pluck up the courage to share our faith, God can feel a million miles from the conversations that you long to have with your friends. And even if they did actually listen to what we said, they would probably just feel like rolling their eyes at our feeble words.

And if we're honest, it's easy to **think that God is a bit irrelevant,** maybe even a bit embarrassing. These days, talking about God seems a bit unintellectual, a bit odd, perhaps even a bit boring. Whatever God is, He isn't something that we feel very comfortable talking about. Sharing our faith can feel like a trip to the dentist: if anything substantial is going to happen, it's unlikely to be a pleasant process. The result of all these feelings is that our evangelism is paralysed by the suspicions that God is weak, God is distant, God is irrelevant. Is that really what God is?

No. All of that is what God is not. **God is actually** *God.* And that's the truth we have to write on our hearts. It's a truth that runs right through the Bible, right through Christian theology and right through the history of God's mission through His church. God is not weak, not distant, not irrelevant.

In fact, if God is God, then it is impossible for Him to be any of these things. The Source of all strength, energy, movement and life, cannot be weak. The Sustainer of every part of the universe, who knows every detail of every person, cannot be distant. And the Absolute of all reality, for whom everything exists and to whom everyone must give an account, can never be irrelevant. If your evangelism is crippled by feelings that God is incapable, absent, or obscure, then you can happily retire from having those feelings. **God is none of those things. God is God.**

One of the best places to see this is in the life of Moses. In Exodus chapter 3, God appears to Moses, who, for the past forty years, had been a shepherd in more or less the middle of nowhere. God speaks to him from a burning bush and tells Moses that he is going to return to Egypt to lead the Israelites out of slavery and into freedom. Moses, understandably, is daunted at the task. Among his fears is the question of how the Israelites (with whom he hasn't lived for four decades) will react. So, Moses says to God, 'If I come to the people of Israel and say to them, "The God of your fathers has sent me to you," if they ask me, "What is his name?" what should I say?' And God gives an outstanding reply:

> God said to Moses, 'I AM WHO I AM.' And he said, 'Say this to the people of Israel, "I AM has sent me to you"' (Exod. 3:14).

God is who He is. That is simultaneously the simplest and most profound theological statement that can ever be made. This is the foundational truth of our all theology, and it's quite amazing how such small and simple words can express the most monumental and profound truths. God is who He is. God is God.

Among many other things, these simple words highlight the uniqueness of God: there is no other. They reveal the personal-ness of God: He has certain qualities, attributes and characteristics. They show the consistency of God: He is always true to His own character. And they reinforce the perfection of God: He has always been, and will always be, everything He is meant to be. The thing that Moses and the Israelites needed to know more than anything else is that God is God. And, when it comes to sharing our faith, that's exactly what we need to know as well.

Four very awesome truths about God

The rest of Moses' story reveals more about who God is. There's a wealth of theological riches in these chapters in Exodus; let me just pick out four truths about God, four truths that are very awesome – awesome in the truest sense of that word.

Number One: God is sovereign. Right through the narrative, from the moment God shows that He knows the circumstances of Moses and the Israelites all the way through to when God demonstrates that He, and not the mighty Egyptian Pharaoh, is the one who is really in control. God is the one who reigns over every person, every location and every moment. God is sovereign.

Number Two: God takes the initiative. He is the one who comes to Moses; He is the one who initiates a work of salvation.

It all starts from Him. The day the bush burned began as a very ordinary day for Moses. He was looking after his sheep; he wasn't looking for a revelation from God. But God takes the initiative and from there everything changes.

Number Three: God is powerful. He has all the resources needed to accomplish His plans. That is seen right before Moses' eyes in the bush that is burning but isn't consumed. God's resources never run out. And in the dramatic departure from slavery, the people of both Israel and Egypt are left in no doubt that God is incredibly powerful.

Number Four: God is compassionate. He has heard the cry of the Israelite slaves; He has seen their suffering; He has remembered His covenant promises, and He is ready and willing to help. God is sovereign; God takes the initiative; God is powerful and God is compassionate. So when God says that He is who He is, that's the kind of thing He means. And we stand before Him in awe.

Four very helpful truths for sharing our faith

But these aren't just four amazing truths about God for us to learn. They are four very helpful truths for sharing our faith. And it is vital that we remember them, because they could not be more relevant to us as we seek to evangelise.

God is sovereign. That means that every single time you speak about your faith with someone, you are doing that under the authority and reign of God. He is the one who is in control. He knows you, He knows the person you are talking to, and there is never a moment when your efforts at evangelism are out of His reach. As you share your faith with your friend, the sovereign hand of God is on your shoulder.

God takes the initiative. Therefore, every time you share your faith, you are simply following God's initiative. You didn't start it, He did. You go because He's sending you. You are there because that's where He's put you. And the whole reason you've got a message to share is because He has given us something to say. When you try to talk about Jesus, you don't need to look over your shoulder wondering whether God is coming with you into the conversation. He is already there, and He is always one step ahead.

God is powerful. That means that every single time you talk about Jesus, your words are backed up by the inexhaustible power of God. Think about the electricity supply in your house. In your rooms, you more than likely have lots of sockets on the walls. We use these to plug in our phone chargers, our TVs, our hair dryers and dozens of other devices. A wee white socket on the wall doesn't look like much; they are a fairly unexciting part of life. If you were visiting a friend's house for the first time, they are probably not going to say, 'Check out the sockets in here,' as they give you the grand tour. But a socket is actually a source of remarkable power. That's because the sockets on your walls are connected to a ring main, which is connected to a fuse box, which is connected to an electricity supply cable which (unless you live in a very remote place!) is connected to a national grid. And that means that the wee socket on your bedroom wall has got the power of every power station, hydro-electric dam, wind farm and solar panel on the national grid connected to it. That is a colossal amount of power. That's why, if you try and empty all the electricity out of the plug on your bedroom wall, you will be waiting a long, long time. That is a picture of what you are like as a Christian sharing your faith. You might feel like a tiny, insignificant socket. But you are connected to the God whose power is phenomenal and which will never, ever run dry.

And **God is compassionate.** Every single time you try to evangelise, you are demonstrating the extraordinary mercy, grace and love of God. You are reaching out on His behalf, you are speaking to someone who God deeply cares about, and any love that you show will just be a glimpse of the love that that person can experience if they come to know God themselves. All four of these truths help us when it comes to sharing our faith. But the key point is that none of them are grounded on who *we* are. They are all grounded on who *God* is.

It is vital to recognise this because, when it comes to sharing our faith, there are a lot of things that we need. That's part of the reason why the task of evangelising seems so intimidating and overwhelming. We need opportunities to arise. We need energy for the task. We need hurdles to be taken down. We need people's eyes to be opened. We need a message that will actually change lives. We need power that goes beyond anything that mere human effort is capable of. Do we have all of that? We don't. But God most definitely does, because God is God.

So is God strong enough to use weak people like you and me? Is God able to open the eyes and soften the hearts of your friends, neighbours, colleagues? Is God going to keep His promise to build His church? Can the Holy Spirit empower people like you to bear witness for Jesus? Is God sovereign and able to overcome opposition? Is God able to do more than we can even ask or think? Of course He is! Why? Because God is *God*. He is not just a force, or a philosophy, or a lifestyle movement, or a guru, or an ideology; He is God. He is bigger, stronger, wiser, more powerful, more compassionate, more capable, more gracious and more loving than anything else in all existence.

And, of course, that also means that we are not God. So we are not able or capable and nor do we need to be. None of that matters because God is God. And to prove that, we only have to look at the history of the church. We look at evangelism today and it seems a near impossible task. And yet God has been making it happen for hundreds of years. Every generation of the church starts with nothing. But in every generation God is bringing people to faith in His Son, Jesus Christ. I once listened to a close friend talking about how he had become a Christian. He spoke about his struggles with alcohol and his wrestling with the gospel for many years. Eventually, he came to faith in Jesus and became a wonderful witness and servant in his local church. But as he recounted the extraordinary change in his life, he concluded by saying, 'And do you know the best bit of it all? God did it.' Of course God did it! You don't need to go to Calvin's great book, *The Institutes of the Christian Religion* to see God's incredible initiative and sovereignty in saving sinners. You can see it in the lives of every Christian around you. You can see it in your own life. For every Christian there has ever been we can say the same thing: God did it. So, as you think of every person around you that you long to see coming to faith, can God do it again? Too right He can. He can do it, because God is God.

So this fact – that God is God – is vital to remember because it is a huge help to us as we seek to share our faith. It should give us several things that we need. **It should give us confidence**: God is able, God is willing, God is sovereign. God has already worked in our lives and in the lives of millions and millions of people, and He has no intention of stopping. Can God work in the life of your friend, or neighbour, or colleague, or family? Absolutely! It is impossible for the answer to that question to be no. Impossible. And, on top of that, the fact that God is God means that every day something amazing might happen. If you look again at Exodus 3, at the start of the chapter Moses was just looking after the sheep. By the end of the day, the history of the world was about to change. As you get up tomorrow morning, just think of all that God can actually do by the time you go to bed tomorrow night.

It should give us a sense of dependence. As we seek to share our faith with others, we do so in complete dependence on the God who alone is God. So if you see your friend and think 'I could never have an impact on their life', then you are right, you can't. But God can. If you see a community around you and think that your church isn't making much progress, that is not a problem for God. That is why in the great commission, when Jesus said 'Go!' He also said, 'I am coming with you!' God is God, so as we seek to bring the gospel to people around us, we do so in total dependence on Him. We are not strong enough, not capable enough, not brave enough, not powerful enough, we are nowhere near sufficient. But God is. God is God. He is with you and it's His work that you are doing.

It should motivate us to obedience. That word 'obedience' raises two very important points. First, sometimes we can slip into the trap of thinking that dependence on God means that we shouldn't really do anything; we should simply wait for God to save people. It is easy to see why you might think like that. However, it is not a biblical approach. The point we have to remember is that our witnessing is not an act of jumping ahead of the God who is sovereign; our witnessing is an act of obedience to the God who is sovereign. In other words, first and foremost, we don't evangelise because we think that we can convert people ourselves. We do it because God has told us to. And if God is God, then surely there can never be any part of our lives where we feel we have the right to disobey Him. Now, of course, any fruit that comes from our efforts is entirely through the work of God the Holy Spirit in and through us. But whether the harvest is great or small is not our primary concern. Our primary concern is that God has commanded us to go out with the gospel. And if we really believe that God is God, then all of His commands must be obeyed. Secondly, the Bible also makes it clear that obedience isn't just *why* we evangelise, it is also a key aspect of *how* we evangelise. At the heart of Christian witness is a daily commitment to think, speak and behave in a way that follows the teaching and example of Jesus. We strive to obey Him, and by doing so everyone around us will know that we are His disciples.

Finally, it should remind us to never, ever give up. If evangelising is one of the hardest parts of being a Christian, giving up on evangelism is one of the easiest. Even if we do finally pluck up the courage to speak to someone or invite them to church, sometimes it can look as though nothing is happening. And when we see little results, we can easily be discouraged and succumb to the temptation to abandon the task. But if God is God, then there is never a reason to give up. Every single person who has ever become a Christian was spiritually blind, deaf, distracted, and possibly not even aware of any kind of problem. And then God came on the scene. If you are surrounded by blind, deaf, distracted people who probably don't even have a clue about the danger they are in, do not for one minute think that you should give up. Every single one of them is an opportunity for God to show you that He is God. And when you hear someone talk about how they became a Christian, one of the wonderful things you often discover is that their journey to faith in Jesus Christ involved many different people, many different sermons, many different conversations, and most of the time the people involved weren't even aware of the contribution that they had made. All the time, the God who is actually God, has been working everything together to bring another precious child into His family.

When it comes to sharing your faith, it is normal to feel weak, it's OK to feel daunted, and it's very likely that you'll feel inadequate. But in the midst of all that, never, ever forget that God is God. We can be so easily discouraged by thinking that the nation is too dark, the church is too weak, the challenge is too great, people's hearts are too hard, the situation is too bleak, and we are too useless. But none of that is true. In fact, all of that is complete nonsense, because God is God!

22

STUDY QUESTIONS:

1. Read Exodus 3. In what ways can you relate to how Moses felt? How does that hinder you in sharing your faith?

2. Are you tempted to think that God is weak, or distant, or irrelevant? In what ways?

3. Think of someone with whom you would love to share your faith. In what ways can the fact that God is God help you do that?

4. How can the fact that God is God shape the way we pray for conversions?

5. 'There's not much point in attempting to evangelise because we can't do anything without the Holy Spirit moving among us.' Is it appropriate to think like that? Why or why not?

6. How has God shown that He is God in your own life?

CHAPTER TWO

The Truth is the Truth

Near where I come from, it is not uncommon to see a sheepdog attached to a tether outside someone's house. A long rope or chain is used to give the dog a little bit of freedom to move around, but the main purpose is to keep the dog confined to a specific area, primarily for its own safety. If the dog tries to run, it's held back. When you walk past a sheepdog on a tether, one of three things tends to happen. One: the dog barks like crazy. This is because it feels threatened and defensive. The dog and you are now in a confrontation. The tether reduces her options, so the default tactic is a whole lot of barking. Two: the dog cowers in fear. She can't run away; she's exposed, afraid of what might happen next. Three: the dog might not be afraid; she might, in fact, be friendly. She tries to come to meet you, cheerfully walking towards you until 'Oomph!', the tether stops her in her tracks. The dog was quite happy until you came along. The moment it meets you, the problems arise and are exacerbated because the dog is held back by the tether.

In our efforts at evangelism, we can very easily feel like a sheepdog tied to a tether. We are quite comfortable as long as we don't actually have to interact with people. But when the opportunities to share our faith do arise, not many of us feel like an eagle soaring through the skies or like a stag bounding over the hills. Most of us feel stuck, held back by a tether, unsure what to say or do. So, like the dog, we might bark. We try to tell people that they are wrong, that they need Jesus, that they need to listen to us. Or we might cower in fear, lying down with a whimper, wishing that we were braver, smarter and more confident. Or maybe we will try and speak, like the dog, we trot forward optimistically, only for doubts, fears and insecurities to yank us back before we've made any real connection. When it comes to evangelism, we long to go forward, we long to do more, but whenever we try to run, something is holding us back.

There are many reasons for this, but one of the most common tethers in evangelism is the question of truth. We believe that the gospel of Jesus Christ is the truth. We want to communicate that truth. We want other people to understand, accept and trust that truth. It sounds so simple. But the question of truth can so easily hold us back. That might be because we can feel that the truth is under threat, so our default interaction with others is confrontation. We need to defend the truth and stop them from damaging the truth because people who don't agree with us are a threat. Or we might be held back by the feeling that with us, the truth is in poor hands. So we shy away from speaking, we're terrified of the question we can't answer, we're pretty sure that someone else would do a far better job. Or, we might be held back by the feeling that the person we want to speak to just doesn't want the truth. So we might come some of the way, we might even form a good friendship, but taking that step to speak about the truth in Jesus is a step too far. We are stopped in our tracks by the feeling that the truth is just not what they want to hear. Even though we believe and know that the gospel is the truth, our evangelism is tethered by the feeling that people can't believe us because we're contradicting their understanding of truth; people won't believe us because we're rubbish at speaking the truth; people don't believe us because they don't really want the truth.

If that is how you feel, then the crucial thing you need to learn is that the truth is *the truth*. And you need to remember that in John chapter 8 Jesus said something wonderful for everyone who feels held back, confined or tethered in their evangelism. What did He say? He said, 'If you abide in my word, you are truly my disciples, and you will know the truth, and *the truth will set you free*.' These words are bursting with amazing theology; Jesus' message leads us into glorious freedom from sin, guilt and death. But these words are also a huge encouragement for us in terms of evangelism. To see that, we need to remind ourselves of three truths about truth.

Three truths about truth

One: Truth is central to life

Over the past 100 years or so, the whole idea of truth has come under scrutiny. Postmodern philosophy has redefined how we understand truth. For centuries, humanity has believed that certain stuff is true, and we need to discover what that truth is. Postmodernism has generally rejected that idea of objective external truth. The idea of a metanarrative is to be avoided. Instead, truth is seen in more relative, subjective and individualistic terms. In other words, the great overarching truth of reality is that there is no great overarching truth of reality. Consequently, what's true for me doesn't have to be true for you. That's been a dominant philosophy in many parts of the world for the past century or so, and you can see it running all the way through society, from the Disney movie that says that anyone can be anything, all the way through to the politician who will spin the truth into whatever best suits their agenda. Today, truth is old fashioned, uncool and maybe even offensive.

Except hardly anyone actually believes that. Despite all the influence of postmodernism in art, music, politics and religion, it is still the case that truth is absolutely central to life. And to prove that, all you need to do is look at the news headlines. So, yes, in the peace and tranquillity of a movie or a song, people might be quite happy with the idea that you can have your truth and I can have mine. But when controversy strikes, everyone wants the truth. In fact, they demand it. The #MeToo movement wants the truth about sexual abuse in the film industry. Black Lives Matter wants the truth about racial inequality. Greta Thunberg wants the truth about climate change. When there's an election or a referendum, the public want the truth about exactly what the results are. When Volkswagen programmed their cars to give a false reading when testing emissions, no one said, 'Och well, truth is relative.' There was international outrage, and VW was given one of the largest fines in corporate history. When it comes to controversy, when it comes to the big issues of life, people still want the truth.

All this forces us back to the fact that truth is inherently and inescapably exclusive. The truth is the truth. And anything that isn't the truth isn't true. Climate change can't be true and a hoax; Trump and Biden can't both have won the election; consent can't be simultaneously obtained by the man and withheld by the woman. Truth forces us to recognise that certain things are fact, certain things are fiction; certain things are right, certain things are wrong; certain things are genuine, certain things are fake. Truth is central to life. The people around you want the truth. They need the truth. They demand the truth. The key question, however, is what is the truth?

Two: Truth is central to the gospel

Why was Jesus born? That's a key question in Christian theology. The whole Bible is centred on the life of Jesus; the fact that He came, lived, died and rose again. But why did He come in the first place? Why was He born? Our instinctive answer to that might be to say that He has come to be the Saviour of sinners; He's come to establish God's kingdom, He's come to give eternal life. All of that is correct. But in John chapter 18, when Jesus was being interrogated by the Roman Governor Pilate, He gives His own answer to the question, 'Why was Jesus born?' Do you know what He said? He said, 'For this purpose I was born and for this purpose I have come into the world ... *to bear witness to the truth*' (John 18:37). Truth is central to Jesus' mission. In fact, the truth is central to Jesus' whole identity. In John 14, He declares that He *is* the truth. That means that, as far as Jesus is concerned, if we want to know the truth, we need to know Him. At the heart of the person and work of Jesus, at the heart of the Christian gospel, is the revelation of truth.

If you read any part of the Bible, you quickly discover that the **truth matters to God.** He is the God of truth (Isa. 65:16), He speaks the truth (Isa. 45:19), His word is truth (John 17:17), He hates a lying tongue (Prov. 6:17) and it is impossible for God to lie (Heb. 6:18). As the Westminster Shorter Catechism says, 'God is infinite, eternal and unchangeable in his ... truth.' God speaks, maintains, propagates and defends the truth. That is why you can trust everything that God says to you, and that's why you can be completely honest in everything that you say to Him. With God, you never need to be afraid that He's conning you by pretending to be something He's not, and you never to fear that you have to con Him by pretending to be someone that you're not.

The devil, in contrast, 'does not stand in the truth, because there is no truth in him. When he lies, he speaks out of his own character, for he is a liar and the father of lies' (John 8:44). And the whole of human history is wrapped up in that tension between the truth that God reveals and the lies that the devil spins. From Adam and Eve all the way through to the newspaper published this morning, the devil has been leading people away from God and into a mess. Satan has convinced humanity that God's commands are restrictive, that God's priorities are irrelevant, that God's requirements aren't urgent. All of these are lies. But the whole of human history is shaped by people who are listening to 'truth' that isn't the truth at all.

In response to that, **God resolves to reveal truth that actually is the truth.** That desire to reveal the truth goes hand in hand with His desire to bring salvation; God 'desires all people to be saved and *to come to the knowledge of the truth*' (1 Tim. 2:4). At the heart of Christianity is the fact that the truth is the truth. Only the truth is the truth. And only true truth can actually save us. God's goal is to reveal that truth to us, and that objective is at the heart of why Jesus came.

But not everyone believed what Jesus said. Far from it. He frequently encountered questions, suspicion and opposition. A great example of this is in John 8. Here, Jesus is speaking with the religious leaders in Jerusalem. In verse 12, Jesus makes the great declaration, 'I am the light of the world. Whoever follows me will not walk in darkness, but will have the light of life.' This is a stunning statement about truth: Jesus brings spiritual illumination, visibility and clarity to the world. But the Pharisees object. They say to Him, 'You are bearing witness about yourself; your testimony is not true.' Jesus responds by telling them:

> Even if I do bear witness about myself, my testimony is true, for I know where I came from and where I am going, but you do not know where I come from or where I am going. You judge according to the flesh; I judge no one. Yet even if I do judge, my judgment is true, for it is not I alone who judge, but I and the Father who sent me. In your Law it is written that the testimony of two people is true. I am the one who bears witness about myself, and the Father who sent me bears witness about me (John 8:14-18).

At first glance, these verses can seem a bit hard to understand. Jesus' argument can sound a little bit circular, maybe even a little bit convenient. The Pharisees are telling Him that if He's the only one making these claims, then they can't believe Him because no one else can corroborate. Jesus replies by saying that He isn't making these claims on His own. He is saying these things because He has been sent by God the Father. His message is the Father's message, the Father and the Son together are both declaring the truth. To the sceptic, that might all sound very convenient. Jesus makes these huge claims and then uses God the Father, whom no one can actually interrogate, as His key witness.

But what if Jesus is actually telling the truth? If Jesus is sent from the Father to reveal the truth and bring light to the world, do we really expect Him to get corroboration from a rabbi or a prophet or a friend? If Jesus has actually come from God the Father, should He appeal to the witness of fallible humans around Him, or to the God of truth who actually sent Him? If Jesus said, 'I am the light of the world, and here's Peter and John, they'll confirm it,' then I would be nervous. But Jesus doesn't do that and He doesn't need to do that. Instead, He relies on the fact that He has been sent by the Father. He relies on the fact that the truth is the truth.

But that still leaves us crying out for an answer to the question, How do we know this is true? Surely anyone can say, 'I have come from God, I have the truth, because God has sent me.' History is full of people making that kind of outrageous claim. What makes Jesus different? Well, this is where Jesus says something absolutely brilliant. He says, 'My testimony is true, because *I know where I have come from and I know where I am going.*' What is Jesus doing? He is grounding His claims on His origin and His destiny. There is an inextricable link between Jesus' origin, Jesus' message and Jesus' destiny. Jesus claims to know where He has come from, He knows that He has been sent by God. But like we said, anyone can do that. The real test is not where someone claims to be from. The real test is where they end up. That's why Jesus doesn't just claim to know His origin. He also claims to know where He is going. His message will lead on to the conclusion. And that conclusion will prove whether or not Jesus' claims really are the truth.

So what were His claims, and what kind of conclusion could validate them? Jesus' claim was that He had come from God to give eternal life to the world. There's only one conclusion that can validate a claim like that. One event can prove His words to be true. If Jesus really has come from God to give eternal life to a dying world and a dying humanity, then there's one thing that has got to happen: a resurrection. If Jesus ends up dead, then His words are empty and all our faith is in vain. If Jesus rises again, then everything He says is verified. Jesus knows His origin and He knows His destiny. If the resurrection happened, then the truth of the gospel really is the truth.

Three: Truth is central to evangelism

But what has all this got to do with sharing our faith? The key point we are trying to get to here is to recognise that **if Jesus' message is true and if we remember that that truth really is the truth, then it can liberate us from the doubts and fears that are holding us back in sharing our faith.** In terms of evangelism, Jesus' words are absolutely right: the truth will set you free.

If the truth is the truth, then that means that we don't need to bark back in confrontation when we interact with those who disagree with us. The gospel doesn't need our shouts to make it true. It's already true. Nothing can change that, nothing can threaten it. Locked away somewhere in Paris is the International Prototype of the Kilogram, a small cylinder of platinum-iridium-alloy that, until 2019, was the reference point which defined the kilogram. In 2019, the definition of the kilogram was changed to a new system of calculations that I don't really understand, but for over 100 years, this lump of metal in Paris was the definition of what a kilogram was. The reason they changed the calculation system was because even though it was locked away, they still couldn't prevent small variations. The true kilogram had to be protected, because it could be so easily compromised.

The gospel is the complete opposite of that. The truth in Jesus is impregnable. So, if you meet someone who disagrees with everything you say, you do not need to panic; you do not need to worry that the foundation of your faith is about to be pulled out from underneath you, and you don't need to go on the attack as if somehow this person's arguments are going to undo the resurrection and topple Jesus from His place at the right hand of God. Instead, you can just talk about the truth. Ask them what they believe, ask them why they believe it, ask them how they know it's true. They might say something you've not thought of before, they might raise questions that you can't answer right there and then, you might need to ask for someone else's input, you might need to do a bit of research yourself. All of that is healthy. But not for one second do you need to be afraid that your Saviour is going to be falsified. The resurrection has happened and it cannot be undone. The truth is the truth. Remembering that can liberate us from feeling intimidated and help us turn a confrontation into a conversation.

If the truth is the truth, that means that you don't need to cower away in silence, afraid that your feeble efforts are going to do more harm than good. All you need to do is tell the truth. Talk about the difference that Jesus has made in your life. Talk about the reality of His peace, the joy of His friendship, the wonder of His love. One of the great things about Christianity is that you don't need to be a genius to be an expert. An expert is simply someone who knows what they are talking about. So you might still have a lot to learn about theology, there are, no doubt, vast areas of the Bible that you're still getting to know, there may be many experiences still ahead of you on your path as a disciple. But in terms of sharing your faith, in terms of telling someone the truth about the difference that Jesus can make in someone's life, you're not a clueless idiot. You are an expert. You're an expert because when we say that Jesus has come to save us, to heal us, and to transform us, you know exactly what that means.

But here, we do have to be very careful. The truth is the truth, so that means we have something to say. But if the truth is the truth, then that must also shape the way that we say it. Ephesians 4:15 reminds us that we must speak the truth, but we must do so in love. Arrogance, harshness, dishonesty and hypocrisy will all undermine our attempts to share the truth. No wonder, because if the truth of Jesus' love doesn't shape the way we speak to others, then it makes it look like we don't really believe the truth that we are trying to share. There may be occasions when people are put off by what we say. Far more likely, however, is that they will be put off by the way we say it. Jesus is the giver of eternal life, indescribable peace, unshakeable hope, and immeasurable joy. The way we speak about that must reflect the fact that what we are saying really is the truth.

And if the truth is the truth, then that means you actually have what the people around you are longing for. It probably doesn't feel like that, but if people want truth (which they do) and if Jesus' message is the truth (which it is) then you never again have to be held back by the thought that people don't want to hear what you are saying. That doesn't mean it will all be plain sailing, it doesn't mean that our every word will be accepted with open arms. But it does mean that we have something amazing to say, something that deep down everyone longs for.

In terms of truth, **there are two things that are particularly brilliant about Christianity. One is that it is so philosophically satisfying.** The Bible doesn't directly explain everything, so it doesn't tell us every truth there is to know about engineering, medicine, mathematics, or biology. Instead, the Bible focuses on certain things. And in particular, it focuses on origin and destiny, just like Jesus did in John 8. And for these two massive questions, Christianity gives us the truth. Christianity tells us that the universe is a creation, made by the God who has the power, resources and wisdom to make and sustain it. That explains why you can stand at the top of a mountain and say 'Wow!' and why, no matter how far you look through a telescope or a microscope, the wonder of what you see will take your breath away. Christianity tells us that, within that creation, humanity is special. We have extraordinary privileges and solemn responsibilities. That explains why so many parts of life are wonderful, which of course is why all the great other discoveries of mathematics, engineering and science are possible. But that also explains why we know that exploitation, betrayal, inequality, abuse and every other awful thing we see around us are all wrong. Christianity explains our origins. But it also confronts us about our destiny. Beyond this life lies eternity, where every one of us will have to give an account of ourselves to God. That explains why, deep down, we long for a day when every injustice is put right. It also explains why, deep down, no one sees death as their friend. Everyone knows that it's an enemy. And without Jesus, it's an enemy that we can't overcome. The Bible gives the truth about our origin and our destiny. But the great tragedy of human history is that we have exchanged the truth of God for a lie, and worshipped the creature rather than our Creator.

The other brilliant thing is that Christianity is so practically relevant. It explains why the truth matters to every one of us. So why is #MeToo an issue? Why is racism so wrong? Why is climate change so serious? It is because men are not animals who can use their strength to do what they like with women; people are equal, all made in the image of God no matter what their race; and the world is a precious gift entrusted to us by God and which we must look after responsibly. The controversies all around us are there because people are crying out for the truth. As Christians, we have it. We have something amazing; we have something that people long for. The next time you feel pulled back by the niggle that people don't want to hear about the gospel, you can undo that tether by remembering that the truth is the truth.

Truth and faith

Ultimately, however, the question of truth is inseparable from the question of faith. No one can claim to know any truth without some kind of faith. At the very least, we have to trust the reliability of our own eyes, ears and thoughts. Discovering the truth will always rely on faith. That's why our great hope is not that people will be persuaded by the truth in Jesus, our hope is that they will be saved through faith in Jesus. Over the centuries, theologians have said that there are three key aspects of faith and they have cool Latin names. *Notitia*: this refers to knowledge. There's a content of information that we need. We can't believe something we don't know about. *Assensus:* that speaks of agreement. If we are going to believe something, we must give our assent. We have to agree that the content of information given to us is accurate. And *Fiducia:* this is talking about trust. We might know a truth, we might agree with it, but to reach the point of faith, we have to commit to the point of trust. As we seek to evangelise, we long for each of these. We long to see people grow in knowledge and understanding of the gospel message. We long to see them accept the reality of who Jesus is and what He has done. And we long for them to trust in Him for themselves, placing all their hope and dependence on Him. If the truth is the truth, then the right response is faith.

But for our evangelism, we also need to apply these three words to ourselves. We need the *notitia* that remembers Jesus' promise to build His church. We need the *assensus* to agree that Jesus really can use people like us. And we need the *fiducia* that trusts Jesus to actually do it, in fact, to do even more than we can ask or think. These are the truths that will help us cut the tether and go and tell people about the amazing difference that Jesus makes in their lives. Because the truth is, when it comes to reaching a lost world, Jesus uses people just like you. That truth, and every truth that Jesus reveals, is the truth. And the truth will set you free.

STUDY QUESTIONS:

1. In what ways do you feel tethered in terms of sharing your faith?

2. Are there questions that you are afraid of being asked? Please share examples.

3. 'You can have your truth and I can have mine.' In what ways have you seen examples of this mindset around you?

4. Do you think people around you are looking for truth? Where do people go for answers? How might the gospel provide the answers they are seeking?

5. Jesus said that He was born to bear witness to the truth (John 18:37). In what ways does Jesus do this? How does the resurrection relate to what Jesus said?

6. Paul says that we are to speak the truth in love (Eph. 4:15). What do we need to do to achieve this and what do we need to avoid?

CHAPTER THREE

Good News is Good News

Today, we are bombarded with a constant stream of news. Gone are the days where we had to wait until we picked up a morning newspaper or tuned in to the News at Ten before we went to bed. The advance of internet, digital TV and mobile technology means that now we can get the news any time we want. You can read your newspaper on a tablet before you get out of bed, you can watch numerous 24-hour news channels, and your phone can give you any amount of news you want, any time you like. Today, we are bombarded with news.

Except that's not quite accurate. **The truth is, today, we are bombarded with bad news.**

If you pick up your phone right now and go to a national or international news website, then I am almost certain, in fact, I am completely certain, that the majority of stories on that site will be reporting bad news. Not all of them will be: hopefully there will be some positive news stories, and these are wonderful. But they are always in the minority. Our daily stream of news is predominantly negative. We are told about inequality: racism, poverty, discrimination and neglect. We're told about injustice: local, national and global news of people exploited and abused through the actions of others. Illness: men, women, young, old, all struck down by disease, injury and depression. Isolation: people separated from loved ones, people left all alone. And we are told about immorality: every day, the news feeds us examples of people saying, doing and experiencing awful things. We live in an age where we are constantly receiving bad news.

Why is that? Why is bad news so prominent? Is it because people are just negative? Actually, no. It's because the world is completely broken. Bad news dominates the news because suffering, pain and hostility are the dominant experience of humanity. History proves that, the news headlines this morning prove that, the bruises and scars on your heart prove that. And from a biblical point of view, that makes perfect sense. We have rebelled against God our Creator. We have rejected His rule over our lives. As a result, the world is cursed, humanity is hostile to God and to one another, and death has intruded as an enemy that none of us can avoid. God created the world to be so good. But we have rejected Him. And in doing so, we've consigned the newsreel of human history to be a continuous feed of predominantly bad news.

In a broken world like that, it is so refreshing, encouraging and pleasing to hear good news. Good news is wonderful to hear. When exam results are good, when a couple we know get engaged, and (with apologies to all non-Scottish readers) when Scotland win, it feels like a burst of energy runs right through us. Good news is wonderful to hear. But good news is also easy to tell. When a baby is born, when someone recovers from cancer, when Andy Murray wins Wimbledon (apologies again, non-Brits), we just can't wait to tell others. Good news is easy to tell.

The best news ever is the gospel of Jesus Christ. God has sent His Son to a broken world and a broken humanity in order to bring salvation. So that means that it will feel like the easiest news of all to tell, yes? No. That's not how it feels at all. Telling our friend the good news about our new job feels so easy. Telling our friend the good news about Jesus feels so hard. So often it feels awkward, tense, strained and unpleasant. I have never forgotten reading the honest recognition of this in Rebecca Manley Pippert's superb book *Out of the Saltshaker* where she astutely, and amusingly, confessed that, 'there was a part of me that secretly felt evangelism was something you shouldn't do to your dog, let alone a friend.'[1] Trying to share our faith can so often leave us feeling like the bearers of bad news.

Why is the greatest news in all of history so hard to tell? Why doesn't it feel anywhere near as easy as telling news of babies, engagements and achievements? There are lots of reasons, and there's no doubt that the devil is throwing far more opposition against the gospel than he is against the good news stories of day-to-day life. But if the gospel is the greatest news ever, how can we avoid feeling that our evangelism is an unwanted intrusion into the lives of people around us? The answer is simple. We need to remember that the good news is *good news*.

Good news. That's what the word gospel means. That's what Christianity is all about. It is the message of God's astonishing intervention into history to bring healing and hope to humanity. It is not boring, depressing, disappointing news. It is absolutely brilliant news! In a world of constant bad news, the message of Jesus is so, so good.

That good news runs through the whole Bible, but a great example of what it is all about is found in Isaiah 52:7. Isaiah was a prophet who lived just over 700 years before Jesus and he spoke powerfully to warn the people of his time about God's judgement and to give the people precious promises about God's salvation. In chapter 52, Isaiah is looking ahead to a time of healing and restoration for God's people. And in verse 7, he gives an amazing summary of what God's good news is all about:

> **Isaiah 52:7** How beautiful upon the mountains are the feet of him who brings good news, who publishes peace, who brings

---

1. Rebecca Manley Pippert, *Out of the Saltshaker and into the World*, revised edition (Nottingham: IVP, 1999), 11.

good news of happiness, who publishes salvation, who says to Zion, 'Your God reigns'.

Looking at this verse, we can see that Isaiah tells us four things about this good news.

Peace

The good news is a message of peace. That means that it is not a message of distress and it is not a threat. There are already more than enough of these in the world around us. That was true in Isaiah's time: the nation was disjointed, there was shocking inequality and injustice in society, and the surrounding nations loomed dangerously large over Israel.

Today, circumstances are different but the same kind of problems abound. People face the trauma of broken relationships, maybe with colleagues, maybe with friends, maybe with family. People are treated unfairly, left bruised and bitter by the behaviour of others. People have pressures breathing down their neck: to achieve at school or work, to look good on social media, to stay healthy, to conform to the expectations of the culture around us. Every day people are attacked by external circumstances giving them reason to fear and by internal anxieties producing a constant stream of worries. Life is full of distress. Life is full of threats. The gospel is not adding to these. The gospel is a message of profound, whole-of-life, peace.

Happiness

The good news is a message of happiness. 'Happy' is a word that can be both helpful and unhelpful in theology. It can easily seem unrealistic, as though we are trying to pretend that life as a Christian is always a bed of roses. It can also seem shallow, if Christianity is just about being 'happy', then there are easier ways we can achieve that.

But neither of these is what Isaiah means. The original Hebrew that Isaiah wrote in literally says, 'who brings glad tidings of good'. 'Good news of happiness' is an excellent translation because one of the key points is that this news is not negative. This news is brilliant. It is the kind of news that makes us shout for joy. And not just joy as in 'I got an A in my exam', joy as in 'the Second World War is over'. All of this is reminding us that the gospel is not a message of misery. It is not depressing. It is not a message intended to beat people down. It is a message telling us that something utterly amazing has happened. The gospel is a message of deep, genuine happiness.

Salvation

The good news is a message of salvation. That means that it is not a message of condemnation. Jesus makes that clear in John 3. The reality of condemnation is already here, the proof of it is in the bad news we get every day. But Jesus wasn't sent to condemn the world. He was sent 'in order that the world might be saved through him' (John 3:17).

Does this mean that we shouldn't talk to people about their sin? Not at all. Talking about the gospel will, at some stage, involve discussing the reality of sin. Even that word 'salvation' tells us that there's a problem that we need to be rescued from. But when we talk about sin, we must always be mindful about what we are trying to achieve. This is where it is so important to remember that the Bible's recognition of our sin is not a criticism, it is a diagnosis. And the difference is crucial. A criticism is trying to harm you; a diagnosis is trying to heal you. The message that we proclaim is not about a God who thinks the worst of the person we are talking to. It is a message that tells our friend that, in God's eyes, they are worth saving. In God's eyes, they are worth dying for. The gospel is not about thinking the worst of people. Because when you think the worst of people, you'll find any reason you can in order to give up on them. But when you think the best of people, you'll find any reason you can in order never to give up on them. The whole reason that we have the gospel is because that is exactly how God thinks of us.

Whether people accept the reality of their sin is out of our hands. Question 87 of the Westminster Shorter Catechism reminds us that both a sense of sin in us and an apprehension of mercy in Jesus are only going to happen by God's grace. Our job is not to hammer people with the reality of how horrendous they are. Our job is to show people that, in a world where so many horrendous things happen, God has come to save us. The gospel is a message of astonishing, spectacular salvation.

Sovereignty

The good news is a message of God's sovereignty. As Isaiah says, 'Your God reigns.' This takes us to the heart of what the gospel is about. The good news of the gospel is that God is sovereign. He has not forgotten us; He has not abandoned us. He is King. He has come to conquer the kingdom of evil, to destroy the power of death and to rescue us from all the ways in which sin is holding us captive. He has come to put things right, and He is calling us to come back to Him. When Jesus began preaching, what did He say? He said, 'The time is fulfilled, and the kingdom of God is at hand; repent and believe in the gospel' (Mark 1:15). The gospel is announcing that the King has come, and victory is His.

But this also takes us to the heart of why the gospel is such good news. God is King. That's crucial, because so much of the bad news we receive comes from bad leadership and from terrible misuse of power. So much pain and suffering comes from this; either nationally, where whole nations are a mess; domestically, where people live in tragic fear of those closest to them; or even personally, where our thoughts and decisions can lead us down paths of crippling anguish.

God is calling us away from all of that. That's what makes the gospel such good news. He is calling us away from a world of inequality to a kingdom where every person is a precious child of God. He is calling us away from a world of injustice into a community where the most important commands are to love God and love our neighbour. He is calling us away from a world that is ill and dying and promising to bring us into a new creation where He will wipe away every tear from our eyes, where death shall be no more, neither shall there be mourning, nor crying, nor pain (Rev. 21:4). He is calling us away from isolation into a beautiful family that stretches across all the nations of the world. He is calling us away from immorality and instead is leading us on a path of holiness, restoring us back to everything that we were originally created to be. In other words, in the gospel, God is undoing everything that makes life rubbish. And most amazingly of all, God is calling us to Himself. He is calling us into a relationship with Him through His Son. That is why Christianity is such utterly brilliant news! And the reason God can do it is because He reigns. He is King. The gospel is a message of His supreme, all-conquering sovereignty.

God's good news

So the gospel is a message of peace, of happiness, of salvation and of God's sovereignty. And it's a whole host of other wonderful things too. This is our message; this is what we want to share. It's not dull, it's not miserable, it's not depressing. We must remember that the good news is good news. But we also need to remember it's not just *our* message. In fact, it's not really our message at all. The gospel that we want to share isn't our good news. The gospel is *God's good news*.

In Romans 1:1, Paul introduces himself with these words:

> Paul, a servant of Christ Jesus, called to be an apostle, set apart for the gospel of God (Rom. 1:1).

When you see a phrase 'something "of" something' in the New Testament, there's usually a decision to be made about how it is to be interpreted. There are two options; the 'of something' phrase is either an objective genitive or a subjective genitive. Objective means that the 'of' refers to something along the lines of 'directed towards'. Subjective means that the 'of' refers to 'coming from', or 'belonging to'. So if we take the phrase 'love of God', that can mean two things. It could be talking about someone's love directed towards God. That would make God the object receiving the love (objective genitive). Or it could mean God's love towards someone. If so, God is the subject showing the love (subjective genitive). How do we know which one is correct? The answer is context. The wider sentence or passage will normally clarify which direction the 'of' is going.

So when Paul talks about the gospel of God, is that an objective or subjective genitive? Does he mean 'the gospel about God' or does he mean 'the gospel that comes from God'? Both of course are true, but our instinct might be to go for the first, the objective genitive, that Paul is set apart for the gospel about God. However, if we carry on a little bit further into verse 3, we discover that Paul says that he is 'set apart for the gospel of God (v. 1) ... concerning His Son, who was descended from David (v. 3).' That tells us that the object of the gospel is His Son; it is about Jesus. If so, then that implies that the 'gospel of God' in verse 1 is subjective. In other words, the good news is *God's good news*.

Why is this obscure chat about grammar important? Well, for two reasons. One is because it means that the information that God wants to share with us is *good news*. This is so easy to take for granted. Think of God in all His majesty, power, supremacy and glory. He is miles beyond anything that we can take in. Not only that, we are minuscule in comparison. Tiny, insignificant and unworthy. But incredibly, this infinite God wants to communicate with us. That communication is only possible because of revelation.

God reveals Himself to us. He does that in general terms through the creation around us; He does that in special detail through the Bible. When we compare ourselves to God, it is an absolute miracle that He would want to bother communicating with us at all. But what is even more amazing is that the message He wants to reveal is His message full of goodness. That's right. The God before whom you are a tiny speck ... He wants to talk to you! And He wants to tell you incredibly good news. The gospel is God's good news.

Thus, the gospel is simultaneously a line of communication and a channel through which goodness is poured out. So imagine standing on your phone underneath a tropical waterfall. That's maybe a strange combination of activities, but it's telling us exactly what God's gospel is all about. You are on the phone, so you are receiving information. And you are under a warm waterfall, so you are being showered with blessing. That's what God is wanting to do. That's why He is revealing Himself. That's what God's gospel is all about.

The second reason why it's important to see that the gospel is God's good news is because it is reminding us that you don't have to make the gospel good. It's already good! It's God's message; it's God's plan; it's God's promises. You don't need to make the news good; it already is. You just need to make sure your transmission of it is accurate. That takes us back to one final lesson from Isaiah 52:7.

Beautiful feet

As we have been saying, this verse gives us a superb summary of what good news is all about. In the New Testament, in the letter to the Romans, Paul refers to this same verse as he speaks about how important it is to share the gospel:

> For 'everyone who calls on the name of the Lord will be saved.' How then will they call on him in whom they have not believed? And how are they to believe in him of whom they have never heard? And how are they to hear without someone preaching?

And how are they to preach unless they are sent? As it is written, 'How beautiful are the feet of those who preach the good news!' (Rom. 10:13-15).

Here, Paul makes it clear that what Isaiah 52:7 teaches us still applies to us as we share the gospel. And the final lesson for us to learn is that when we share the good news of Jesus, we are doing something beautiful. Most of the time, we don't feel like that. It is so easy to feel repulsive. But you're not. If you are sharing the good news of Jesus, then you are doing an incredibly beautiful thing. Or as Isaiah says, you have beautiful feet.

But why feet? There are two things that come to mind. First, feet on a person walking across mountains in 730 B.C. are not going to be pretty. They will be very dirty, probably scratched, maybe even bleeding, and definitely not looking like they've just come out of a foot spa. But they are still beautiful. They are beautiful because they are carrying a wonderful message. And that tells you that your efforts to share the gospel don't need to be super-polished models of perfect eloquence and persuasion. They might in fact be a bit messy. But if you are telling people God's good news, if you are conveying it accurately, then you are doing something very beautiful. This is where it's important to remember that you are not going to ruin someone's day if you share the gospel with them. Bad news will ruin someone's day. It feels like a bus has crashed into your stomach when you receive news that's bad. The gospel isn't going to do that. That doesn't mean that everyone will be ecstatic every time we speak about Jesus. But if you share the good news of Jesus with your friend with love, joy, humility and kindness, do you really think that that will wreck their day?

Secondly, 'feet' speaks of movement, action. It is reminding us that as we share the good news, our words are always accompanied by our actions. That's why it's crucial that our presentation of the good news is never accompanied by bad conduct. Good news cannot be carried by bad behaviour. So we should think about our tone – should good news come with exasperation or with enthusiasm? We should think about our gestures – should good news come with a scowl or a smile? We should think about our demeanour – should good news come with harshness or gentleness? We should think about our mindset – should good news come with guilt or with joy? I am not saying that you need to put these on and pretend to be something you're not; that's just hypocrisy. What I am saying is that, if these aren't there, then you need to go back and re-assess your understanding of the gospel. Because if your theology is leaving you exasperated, scowling, harsh and guilty, then your theology is wrong. Orthodox, reformed theology and effective, beautiful evangelism are both grounded on the fact that the good news is *good news*. Tomorrow will be another day full of bad news. In the midst of all that, you have got something utterly brilliant to say.

STUDY QUESTIONS:

1. What bad news have you heard this week?

2. What types of good news do you find easy to share?

3. When you think about sharing the gospel, do you feel that you are sharing bad news or good news? In what ways?

4. What are some of the specific ways in which the gospel is good news, both as described in Isaiah 52:7 and in the rest of Scripture?

5. Think of the bad news you have heard this week. In what ways does the gospel enable us to bring good news to people in these situations?

6. Think about your tone, demeanour, gestures and mindset in sharing your faith. How should the reality of good news influence these?

Chapter Four

Grace is Grace

◇◇

Right then, let's start with a big question: Is your theology Reformed? You might say, 'Yes!' For many of us, that is the theology we have grown up with. For some, we may have come to Reformed theology from a different background. Others, however, might say 'No!' And there are many committed followers of Jesus who don't agree with everything that Reformed theology teaches. But maybe the most likely answer to that question is, 'I think so, but I am not completely sure what Reformed theology actually is.'

If that is your answer, then a good follow up question to ask is this: Are you saved by your own good works? It is very easy to think that the answer to that question is yes. Many people do. A survey of world religions will reveal an oft-repeated pattern; if we want to be saved, or accepted, or enlightened, there are certain good works that we have to do. And many people think that Christianity says the same thing. When my son was in his first year of High School, his Religious Education teacher told the class that Christianity states that if you do good works, then you will go to heaven. And no doubt it is true that in the history of the Christian church, many people have said that the answer to this question is yes, we are saved by our good works.

51

Reformed theology says 'No.' Well, actually, Reformed theology shouts, 'No!' as loud as it possibly can. Prior to the Reformation, many people across Europe understood Christianity to be saying that certain works, certain rituals, certain ecclesiastical requirements were all necessary for salvation. The reason most people thought that was because that was what most of the churches taught. But Martin Luther, John Calvin, John Knox and their fellow Reformers all argued that a theology based on works is a false gospel. They did that because they rediscovered that Christians are never saved by good works. They are only ever saved by God's amazing grace.

So Reformed theology stands on the foundational principle that Christianity is not a works-based religion. It is never about us working our way up to God by proving that we are good enough. Instead, Reformed theology teaches that our salvation is entirely, and only, the result of God's grace. That grace is received by faith; faith alone without any works added. That faith is centred on Christ alone; on who He is and what He has done. All of that is what Scripture teaches, and Scripture alone is where we discover what we are to believe and what God expects of us in response. And because it is entirely reliant on the grace of God, through faith in Christ, as He is revealed in the Bible's unique revelation, all the glory goes to God alone. At the heart of Reformed theology is the astonishing truth that we are saved, not by works, but by grace.

Now let me ask you another question: Is your understanding of evangelism Reformed? You might say, 'Well, yes' especially if your answer to the first question was, 'Yes.' But are you sure? Is it really? I ask that because this is something that I have got wrong again and again. If someone came to me and said, 'I can't become a Christian, I am not good enough,' then I would instantly reply, 'Not true! That's never true. We are saved by grace alone. Being good enough has nothing to do with it.' And that is true. But if someone else came up to me and said, 'You can help many people come to faith in Jesus,' my instinctive reply would be, 'No, I don't think so.' 'Why not?' asks my friend. My reply: 'Because I am not good enough.'

That right there is a description of a Reformed view of theology coupled to a totally unreformed view of evangelism. If I think like that, and if you think like that, we need to remember that when it comes to salvation, *and* when it comes to evangelism, grace is grace.

What is grace?

Grace is central to the Christian gospel. This is made clear in many passages in the Bible. In Romans 3, Paul says that 'all have sinned and fall short of the glory of God, and are justified by his grace as a gift, through the redemption that is in Christ Jesus' (Rom. 3:23-24). In Ephesians 1, Paul declares that 'In him we have redemption through his blood, the forgiveness of our trespasses, according to the riches of his grace' (Eph. 1:7). And in the very next chapter, Paul writes these amazing words:

> But God, being rich in mercy, because of the great love with which he loved us, even when we were dead in our trespasses, made us alive together with Christ – by grace you have been saved – and raised us up with him and seated us with him in the heavenly places in Christ Jesus, so that in the coming ages he might show the immeasurable riches of his grace in kindness toward us in Christ Jesus. For by grace you have been saved through faith. And this is not your own doing; it is the gift of God (Eph. 2:4-8).

And there are tons more.At the very heart of the gospel is grace. But what exactly does grace mean?

When you hear that word grace, what is the first thing that comes into your mind? A prayer of thanks before a meal? The hymn 'Amazing Grace'? Or maybe you think of a person you know who is called Grace. It is totally OK to think of these things, because grace is a word that appears in lots of different contexts. But when it comes to being saved by grace, one of the first things that should come into your mind is that grace is referring to a gift. In fact, the Greek word for grace (*charis*) is almost identical to the Greek word for a gift (*charisma*). And this emphasis on a gift highlights two crucial things: Grace involves a giver and grace involves a receiver.

In terms of our salvation, this giver-receiver relationship is crucial. But how does it work? Our instinct might be to think that we give and God receives. That's what the saved-by-works approach of many religions requires; we have to give good things to God and hope that He will receive them favourably. But what makes Christianity unique (and utterly amazing!) is that it says the exact opposite. The giver is God, the receiver is you, along with every other believer in Jesus Christ.

From our side, the gift is freely received. By 'freely', we mean that it is not earned, prompted, or paid for by us. We don't initiate the giving, we do not (and cannot) do anything to deserve it. It costs us nothing. It is placed in our empty hands. It is a gift freely received.

From God's side, the gift is freely given, but here 'freely' means something different. It doesn't mean 'freely' as in 'no cost'. It means 'freely' as in 'of His own initiative'. In other words, God is not prompted, pestered or persuaded by us to give us grace. He does it freely. It all comes from Him.

But what is even more astounding is that the cost to Him is immense. For us, grace is free. For God the Father, grace comes at the price of His own beloved Son. Sometimes in the news, we hear of corporate acquisitions that come at astronomical cost. The most expensive I can find is the 1999 purchase of Mannesman by Vodafone for $183 billion (that's $284 billion today when adjusted for inflation). But never forget that the most expensive transaction in history was the price that God the Father paid so that you could freely receive His saving grace. As Paul says, our redemption is through His *blood* (Eph. 1:7).

But grace becomes even more amazing when we think about its antecedent and consequence, in other words, what comes before it and what comes after it. Grace's antecedent, what makes it happen, is not our prompting. The antecedent is God's determination to show us favour. The gift is given because God wants it to be given. If you read through Ephesians chapter 1, again and again you are told about God's choice (v. 4), God's will (vv. 5 and 9), God's wisdom (v. 8), God's purpose (v. 9), God's plan (v. 10). It is His idea, His initiative, His choice. So although grace is never prompted by us, that doesn't mean that it isn't prompted by anything. The truth is, grace has the greatest prompting of all. It is prompted by the wisdom, plan and choice of God Himself.

The consequence of this is that we receive undeserved enrichment. This is a key aspect of what grace means. It is a gift that is totally undeserved. It is never, ever earned. If it is earned, then it is not grace. But not only is it undeserved, it is also astounding in its generosity. The gift isn't a little bonus like a free meal or holiday. The gift is utterly astonishing. It is massive. As Paul says in Ephesians 2, it is a gift of immeasurable riches.

So grace is a gift. A gift that we could never demand, but which God is determined to give. A gift that God has deliberately planned, but which results in far more than we could ever have dreamed.

But there's even more. Why is it that God is so determined to show us favour? Why on earth would He do this? The answer is because behind His determination to show us favour lies His eternal love. If you look again at Ephesians 1, you see that it speaks of this so powerfully when it says that

> In love he predestined us for adoption as sons through Jesus
> Christ, according to the purpose of his will, to the praise of his

glorious grace, with which he has blessed us in the Beloved. In him we have redemption through his blood, the forgiveness of our trespasses, according to the riches of his grace, which he lavished upon us, in all wisdom and insight (Eph. 1:4b-8).

This is ultimately where grace takes us back to; the eternal love of God. And as verse 8 tells you, the ultimate consequence of it all is that His love is lavished upon us. Lavished! – what a wonderful word! We receive, enjoy and marvel in God's everlasting kindness. It is all 'so that in the coming ages he might show the immeasurable riches of his grace in kindness toward us in Christ Jesus' (Eph. 2:7).

Once upon a time, I was an engineer and, ever since, I have always found it helpful to draw diagrams. So here's a diagram that captures everything we are trying to explain:

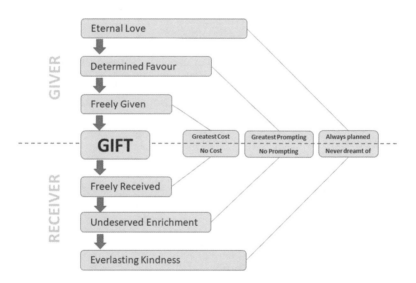

Grace is a gift. It is from God, to us. For the receiver, it involves no payment; for the giver, it requires the greatest payment. For the receiver, we offer no prompting; for the giver, it is initiated by the greatest prompting. God's determination to show us favour results in our undeserved enrichment. His eternal love makes us the recipients of His everlasting kindness. Our endless neediness is met by His amazing grace. Grace is never earned. Grace is never bought. Grace is never deserved. Grace is grace.

Grace and evangelism

Grace, then, lies at the heart of understanding the gospel. It is at the core of our salvation, it is central to Reformed theology. But what we must also remember is that grace doesn't just lie at the heart of understanding the gospel. It also lies at the heart of *sharing* the gospel.

One of the things that Paul makes very clear in Ephesians 1 and 2 is that grace runs right through our salvation, from as far back into the past to as far into the future as we can look. Looking back, the believer's predestination for adoption is to the praise of His glorious grace (Eph. 1:5-6). Looking forward, the promised inheritance awaiting us will reveal 'the immeasurable riches of his grace' (Eph. 2:7). That tells us that every link of the chain in your salvation is all a matter of grace. And that has a crucial implication for evangelism. It means that in terms of your own conversion, the person or people who were used by God to share the gospel with you were all an aspect of God's grace in action. But that also means that if you now go on to share your faith with others, then that is simply an outworking of God's grace as well. And that means that your strength, courage, abilities, confidence and good-enough-ness are irrelevant. Totally irrelevant. Evangelism is all about grace. And grace is grace!

We evangelise by grace

This has three crucial lessons for us. The first is that **grace equips us for sharing the gospel**. We evangelise by grace. When we think of Paul, we think of one of the greatest, if not *the* greatest, evangelists in the history of the church. He went from place to place, city to city, preaching the gospel, planting churches, sharing his faith in synagogues, markets, streets and houses. He saw an astonishing number of people, from all sorts of backgrounds, coming to faith in Jesus. As we think of all that, we can find ourselves asking the question, how did he do it? How was he able to speak, to discuss, to reason, to persuade? How on earth did he do it?!

Well, Paul actually tells us, and his answer is beautiful:

> Of this gospel I was made a minister according to the gift of God's grace, which was given me by the working of his power. To me, though I am the very least of all the saints, this grace was given, to preach to the Gentiles the unsearchable riches of Christ (Eph. 3:7-8).

He did it by grace. He says the same thing in 2 Corinthians when he says that 'our boast is this, the testimony of our conscience, that we behaved in the world with simplicity and godly sincerity, not by earthly wisdom but by the grace of God, and supremely so toward you' (2 Cor. 1:12).

Paul is absolutely explicit that any success in his evangelistic work did not come from his own wisdom, power or confidence. In fact, if anything, Paul makes it clear that he lacked all of those things. Instead, Paul tells us that all of his evangelism was by God's grace. That means that his achievements were not earned, deserved or prompted. They were all a result of what God did by His grace.

Ah, you might think, but that was Paul. He and others had a special gift. He had grace that we don't have. That is true in one sense, there are people with a particular gift in evangelism. But that's not the only truth the New Testament gives us about grace. Later, in 2 Corinthians, Paul makes it clear that God's equipping grace is not confined to Paul or to a select few. Instead, Paul insists that 'God is able to make all grace abound to you, so that having all sufficiency in all things at all times, you may abound in every good work' (2 Cor. 9:8). That verse is magnificently broad in its scope. 'Every good work' includes more than evangelism. But we need to remember that it still includes evangelism! God is able to make grace abound in you in order to do that wonderful work.

This is where our view of evangelism has got to be in line with the rest of our Reformed theology. Are you going to be used by God to help someone come to faith in Jesus because *you* have done good works that qualify you for the task, or because *you* have the kind of 'better' skills that are more impressive to God, or because *you* have somehow earned the right to be one of these super-Christians who are evangelists? Or are you going to share your faith in the full knowledge that, from start to finish, anything that leads to the salvation of your friend is entirely and forever dependent on God's grace? It's all a crucial reminder that when you say, 'I can't share my faith,' you are not actually saying something about yourself. You are saying something about God. And you're not complimenting Him. You are saying that He can't do it. That is never true. He can, because grace is grace.

We evangelise with grace

Secondly, grace doesn't just equip us for evangelism, **grace instructs as to how we should do it.** Colossians 4:2-6 is in many ways a manual for sharing our faith. It gives a beautiful balance that recognises both our utter dependence on prayer and the vital task we have been given to speak. Look at what Paul says:

> Continue steadfastly in prayer, being watchful in it with thanksgiving. At the same time, pray also for us, that God may open to us a door for the word, to declare the mystery of Christ, on account of which I am in prison – that I may make it clear, which is how I ought to speak. Walk in wisdom toward outsiders, making the best use of the time. Let your speech always be gracious, seasoned with salt, so that you may know how you ought to answer each person (Col. 4:2-6).

That is a wonderful handbook for evangelism and one of the key things it tells us is that, as we speak to people about Jesus, our speech must always be gracious. In other words, we must evangelise with grace.

So go back in your minds to what grace means. Grace means giving a gift to a recipient. A gift that isn't paid for. A gift that isn't earned. A gift that is totally undeserved. A gift that is immeasurably kind. If our speech is going to be gracious, then that means that everything we say, both in terms of *what* we say and *how* we say it, must reflect the astonishing beauty of God's grace. In other words, the message *of* grace must be communicated *with* grace.

Or to put it another way, if you want to evangelise badly, then just do it without grace. And that is very easily done. So someone doesn't want to listen; therefore, we respond by losing patience. It's what they deserve. Someone's life is in a bigger mess than you ever thought, so you keep your distance. It's what they deserve. Someone responds well but then slips back, so we move on. It's what they deserve. Someone believes in a whole host of things that go against Scripture, so we wait until they've put their house in order. It's what they deserve. People like that don't deserve grace.

It is so easy to think like that. But if we do, then our theology is drastically unreformed and it is catastrophically wrong. Because what 'they deserve' has got absolutely nothing to do with it. Deserved grace is not grace. Grace is never deserved. And if we evangelise without grace, then we will quickly become frustrated, impatient and disillusioned. But if we share our faith with grace, then we will keep gently talking to the person who doesn't want to listen, we will stand by people no matter how much of a mess they are in, we will go after the person who has slipped back, we will build up a friendship with the person whose worldview is totally different to ours. Why? Because grace is grace, and they desperately need it. An acid test for all of us in sharing our faith is whether or not the immeasurable kindness of God's grace can be heard in both *what* we say and *how* we say it.

We evangelise because of grace

Finally, **the whole reason we evangelise is because of grace**. And that is true no matter where we look. If you look up to God, you see the inventor of grace, the source of grace, the giver of grace, the one who gave His only Son in order that we might be saved by His grace. If you look at the people around you, you see people totally undeserving of grace, people in desperate need of grace, people who deep down are longing for all that grace can give them. And if you look in the mirror, you are not seeing a rubbish evangelist exempt from grace. You are seeing exactly the kind of person through whom God in His grace can do wonderful things.

So let me ask you again, is your understanding of evangelism Reformed? An unreformed view of evangelism will say things like this:

'There's no way I can share the gospel with someone this week.' Grace says, 'You can.'

'I've tried inviting them a hundred times and they keep saying no.' Grace says, 'The 101st try is worth it.'

'I tried speaking to someone and it didn't go well.' Grace says, 'Don't give up. Ever.'

'That kind of person doesn't come to our church.' Grace says, 'No matter how much of a mess they are in, this is exactly where they belong.'

When it comes to evangelism, we must remember that grace is grace. Or as Paul might say, when it comes to sharing your faith with an unbeliever this week, 'It is by grace they will be saved. It is not your own doing. It is the gift of God.'

STUDY QUESTIONS:

1. What are some of the key features of Reformed theology?

2. How might you define grace?

3. Are you tempted to think that you aren't good enough for evangelism? How can grace help you think differently?

4. Can you think of examples of 'evangelising' without grace? How can we guard against these?

5. How does grace contrast to the way people behave in the world around you? How might this give us opportunities to share our faith?

6. Read Colossians 4:2-6 again. If this is an instruction manual for sharing your faith, how might you apply what it says in the week ahead?

Chapter Five

Eternity is Eternity

We all have things that we are afraid of. For some, it's spiders; for others, it's snakes; maybe for you, it's planes or even just heights in general. Lots of things can frighten us. For me, it's scary movies. I hate them. I have never watched a horror film and never will, and I never enjoy scary moments in other types of movie. The creepy toys underneath the neighbour's bed in *Toy Story* are pretty much my limit. Anything beyond that and I am just not going to watch.

These fears can feel very real, yet when we think about it, we are probably blowing things out of proportion. I have seen a lot of people over-react when in the presence of a tiny spider which is just minding its own business, and I probably have to admit that my fear of scary films is a little bit unnecessary. And when compared to many of the awful things that people in the world have actually experienced, the things we are afraid of are often not nearly as big or as scary as we think.

When it comes to sharing our faith, there is something that I think almost all of us are scared of. I am scared of it, I have heard many other people admit that they are scared of it, and I am fairly certain that you will be scared of it too. This is probably the one thing that makes sharing our faith so difficult. This is the one thing we all dread. What are we scared of? We are scared of a moment.

A moment. That moment. The moment when we speak to our friend about our faith, when we try to ask them about what they believe, when we invite them to a church service or Bible Study, *that* moment is terrifying. A good way to test this is to think of someone you know, in your family or a friend, neighbour or colleague, and then put this book down and go and share your faith with them. How does that make you feel? Strong and energised? Or slightly terrified? If it's the former then that is wonderful; may that never change. If it's the latter, then welcome to the club.

Sharing our faith involves a moment that is very likely to fill us with fear and dread. There are lots of reasons for that. We are afraid that it is going to be an awkward moment. Talking to someone about football or the weather or a movie (non-scary I hope!) feels so easy. But talking about Jesus, even to people that we are normally completely comfortable around, feels so tense and difficult.

We are afraid because it is a risky moment. That's what makes it so scary, the fear of what might happen. Will I spoil a friendship? Will I offend the person? Will I get tied in knots? Will I make a hash of it? There's an awful lot of risk in that moment. The fear of what might go wrong can be crippling.

We are afraid because it is likely to be a costly moment. Talking about our faith means exposing ourselves to all the possible outcomes of that conversation. We need to be open, honest and vulnerable. We might be asked difficult questions. We will probably have to follow up with more conversations. We need to be committed to building up a closer relationship with the person in front of us. We have to be both courageous and gentle, patient and bold. All of that takes effort. All of that makes the moment loom all the larger.

The result of the combined awkwardness, risk and cost of the moment is that all too often we conclude that moment just isn't worth it. I have done that so many times in my life. Sometimes, it's the result of lots of thinking; so I plan to speak to someone, but then I have second thoughts because it's going to be awkward, I start to weigh up all the risks in my mind, I become more and more conscious of the cost, so I retreat back to the safe territory of not saying anything at all. Other times, it can be the result of split-second thinking. A door opens for a conversation about the gospel with someone, but instantly the red warning lights labelled 'awkward', 'risky', 'costly' are flashing, and the door closes again as the person or the conversation moves on. I can think of so many occasions in my life when I have shied away from speaking about Jesus because I have been too scared of what a moment might bring.

What is the answer? How do we stop that 'moment' from being such a huge hurdle? Well, we need to find a way of recognising that the moment is not nearly as huge as we think. And the way to see that is to compare it with something bigger. Something much bigger. We need to compare the moment with eternity. And we need to learn that a moment is actually just a moment. Eternity, on the other hand, is eternity.

That comparison between a moment and an eternity is crucial, and it's one that the Bible encourages us to make. In 2 Corinthians 4, Paul writes:

> For this light momentary affliction is preparing for us an eternal weight of glory beyond all comparison, as we look not to the things that are seen but to the things that are unseen. For the things that are seen are transient, but the things that are unseen are eternal (2 Cor. 4:17-18).

These verses move our focus away from the moments of the here and now and direct our attention to eternity. Paul does the same in Romans 8 when he speaks of how 'the sufferings of this present time are not worth comparing with the glory that is to be revealed to us' (Rom. 8:18). And in Philippians 1, he writes about his desire to enter eternity and be with Jesus, which, in Paul's eyes, is 'far better' (Phil. 1:23). The Old Testament Psalms do the same thing. Our lives are like grass or flowers which grow and flourish but then they are gone. God and His steadfast love, on the other hand, are from everlasting to everlasting (Pss. 90 and 103). The Bible frequently takes the moment we are currently experiencing, or that we are about to experience, and compares it with eternity. We need to do the same. But in order to do so, first of all we need to have a clearer understanding of what eternity actually is.

What is eternity?

Eternity is a fascinating subject. It is something that we can't grasp, can't understand, can't fully explain. All our experience is within the boundaries of time, which makes it impossible for us to put eternity, or a piece of eternity, on a table or under a microscope in order to examine it. We can't draw it, model it, or replicate it. It is in a category all of its own. Eternity is beyond what we can comprehend. And yet at the same time, without eternity, nothing else makes sense.

That is because ultimately, all explanations for reality come down to a choice between 'something' or 'nothing'. So, if you look at yourself, are you something or nothing? I am pretty confident you will say that you are something. The alternative is impossible to believe, both because you are clearly not nothing and because if you were nothing you wouldn't be able to say that you were nothing. Is the book in your hand something or nothing? It's obviously something. More widely, is the universe something or nothing? The answer has to be something. Is time something or nothing? Again, it has to be something. Do you see the pattern? If you start from yourself and go all the way to the immensity of the cosmos or the longevity of history and ask, 'Is this something or nothing?' the answer is always the same.

But what if we put time and space together as a single entity with an origin and a destiny and ask, 'Is the ultimate explanation for all this something or nothing?' In other words, is the absolute of reality something or nothing?

What I hope that you can see is that saying 'nothing' to that question is just as preposterous as it is to say 'nothing' when asking the same question about yourself. Just because we tend to put the something/nothing choice a long way away from us, doesn't resolve the issue that our existence makes no sense if we make 'nothing' of our chosen explanation for it all. This explains why there is a sense of eternity in every single one of us. We cannot escape the fact that there has to be something. Something beyond space and time. And that something is called eternity. But what is it?

When defining eternity, there are two key categories to bear in mind. The first is *quantity*. **Eternity is the realm of infinite quantity.** In other words, it's really, really, really big! In the early centuries of the Christian church, there were many great theologians. These thinkers tackled some of the biggest questions about God and reality. Often their studies took them to the limits of what human language can convey, which led them to use a method called the *via negativa*. The basic idea of this is that some things were easier explained in terms of what they are not, rather than in terms of what they are. There are pros and cons to this approach, but it's a good starting point for describing the sheer quantity of eternity.

So, eternity has no beginning. That's instantly beyond what we can fully grasp. In our minds we want to go back to a start, but as soon as we reach it we have to go back further, and further still, and further beyond that. But eternity has no beginning. There was never a period before it. Secondly, eternity has no end. Looking back, there is no start; looking forward, there is no finish. Just on and on and on. Eternity is everlasting, never ceasing, always continuing forever. Thirdly, eternity cannot be measured. No matter how far we stretch back or forward in time, no matter how big we try to picture the eternal realm with the universe and time somewhere within it (however that even works?!), we can't measure it. Metres, miles, mega-watts, light-years; all of them are inadequate. It's too big, too long, too vast. It is immeasurable. And fourthly, eternity cannot diminish. So there isn't a tiny bit less eternity tomorrow than there was today. There's no finite-ness to it. It's infinite. But that word, like all the others, is simply telling us what it's not.

The second key concept, however, is *quality*. Here, we can move beyond the *via negativa*. **There is a qualitative aspect to eternity.** This takes us to one of the many subjects where the teaching of the Bible is so beautiful and so satisfying. If eternity is that never-beginning, never-ending realm that we all ultimately exist within, what is it like? Is it good or bad, static or dynamic, material or spiritual? What qualities does it have?

History has given lots of suggested answers to this. One has been to say that eternity boils down to a material thing. So for centuries, the universe was seen as eternal; the material stuff of the cosmos has always been and will always be. Human life and experience is a blip in the middle of that, but the long-term absolute of existence is material stuff. Another suggestion is that eternity is spiritual but impersonal. So, there is an immaterial force, or cause, or power, from which everything else is derived, towards which everything is moving. There's 'something' out there. Others have seen eternity as a cycle, so although to us reality looks to be moving from past to future, that is actually within a realm that just keeps going round and round and round. So what is eternity like? What is it all about? Some have suggested material stuff, some have proposed an impersonal force, some have argued for a perpetual cycle. And in terms of quality, none of these are particularly appealing.

The Bible gives a different answer to all of these. **According to the Bible, eternity is all about relationship.** So instead of eternity being characterised by a single material entity or force or cycle, the Bible's Absolute of eternity is God. He is the one who is infinite, eternal and unchangeable. But that God is not an isolated being of solitary alone-ness. That God is an eternal relationship of Father, Son and Holy Spirit. That is a relationship of indivisible unity; one God and no other. But it is also a relationship of beautiful plurality; Father, Son and Spirit in perfect fellowship, companionship and love.

From that Absolute comes everything else that exists. All material, all energy, all movement, all coherence, all consciousness, all knowledge, all morality, all love. God is the eternal Absolute of all reality: He stands distinct from His creation; He is the starting point, the reference point and the finishing point for everything. And His eternal existence is in a beautiful, perfect, triune relationship: God the Father, God the Son and God the Holy Spirit.

This is crucial, and wonderful, for two reasons. First, because it tells us that the very foundation and destiny of reality is not explained in terms of a blob of stuff or an unknowable force. Instead, **at the heart of reality is a personal, wise, ethical, loving God.** That explains why every single one of us knows that that love and truth and right and wrong all matter far, far more than material stuff or impersonal forces. But secondly, the fact that relationship lies at the heart of eternity means that **our eternal destiny is entirely determined by the condition of** *our relationship* **with Him** – with the triune, relational God from which everything else comes. And this is where we realise that the question of eternity is not a question of theories or ideas that are way above our heads. The question of eternity is a question that every single one of us has to reckon with. It is a question of life and death. Eternal life or eternal death.

Eternal life

Eternal life – that's the great promise of the gospel. Jesus, the Son of God, has come so that whoever believes in Him might not perish but have eternal life. And at the heart of that eternal life is one thing: knowing God. Jesus makes that clear in John 17:

> When Jesus had spoken these words, he lifted up his eyes to heaven, and said, 'Father, the hour has come; glorify your Son that the Son may glorify you, since you have given him authority over all flesh, to give eternal life to all whom you have given him. And this is eternal life, that they know you, the only true God, and Jesus Christ whom you have sent' (John 17:1-3).

This is so important. God is not just the giver of eternal life; He is the very essence of eternal life. Eternal life is knowing Him. And that doesn't just mean knowing about Him. That means being in a relationship with Him. Eternal life means knowing God the Father as your own Father, knowing God the Son as your Saviour and Brother, and knowing God the Holy Spirit as your Comforter and best Friend.

And the key point is that the quantity and quality of that relationship is just immeasurable. Through Jesus, we can know God. Forever. So we will know His company, His care, His kindness, His creativity, His majesty, His beauty, His glory. And that will never stop. Unsurpassable quality, never-ending quantity.

So for eternity, God will provide for you. There will be a new heaven and a new earth, where everything that is brilliant about the current earth will be even better, and everything that's awful will be gone. For eternity, God will protect you. There will never be a moment when you are exposed, or vulnerable or exploited. For eternity, God will satisfy you. We are made for Him, so we are at our most content and complete when we are with Him. His embrace is the place where we belong more than anywhere else. For eternity, God will delight in you. So we stand in awe of Him, gazing forever at His indescribable majesty. And yet the only reason we love Him is because He first loved us. And, best of all, for eternity, we will *know Him*. Forever and ever, you, and every other Christian, will enjoy a beautiful, eternal relationship with God.

Eternal death

But eternal life is not the only possibility. Eternal life depends on knowing God. It depends on a relationship with Him. For those who do not know God, eternity will mean eternal death. That doesn't mean death in terms of non-existence. It means death in terms of separation. Separation from God, separation from all that is good and beautiful, separation from all hope and peace. An eternity of agonising separation.

Sometimes people think that heaven and hell will be contrasting versions of the same kind of thing. Heaven will be the place where we can be together and everything is good and wholesome and pure. Hell will be the place where we can still get together, but it will be naughty and raucous and wild. So heaven will be like a peaceful walk in the park; hell will be like a reckless night on the town. And I've heard people say that, wherever they end up, they'll have friends in either place.

That idea of hell is terrifyingly inaccurate. Hell is not a place where we do a naughty version of the good stuff in life. Hell is the place where there will be an intensified and relentless experience of everything that is awful. The devil is not wanting to give you a naughty version of heaven that will be bad but still fun. The devil wants to entice you, deceive you and destroy you. He wants you to reject God and to align yourself with his kingdom. That will leave your relationship with God eternally ruined. Instead of enjoying God's eternal blessing, we will fall under His holy wrath.

What will that be like? I can't give a full explanation, and I am not sure I would want to. But the place where we get the clearest glimpse of this is on the cross. There, Jesus took our sins upon Himself. In doing so, He came under the wrath of God. In those moments, He experienced the reality of separation from God. He experienced hell itself as He cried, 'My God, my God, why have you forsaken me?' (Matt. 27:46). There is great mystery involved

71

in that, but one thing that is not mysterious at all is that the cross was horrific. The cross is where we see just how awful eternal death in hell will be. But even in the horror of the cross, we also see the glory of the gospel. That's because the one place you can get a glimpse into what hell is like is to look at the Son of God bleeding and dying so that you don't need to go there. That's why, if we end up in hell, we will only ever have ourselves to blame.

Eternity is inescapable. Through faith in Jesus, eternal life is offered and given freely. Through rejecting Jesus, eternal death is provoked and administered justly. These are the only two options for how we will spend eternity. And eternity is eternity.

Re-assessing the moment

With all of that in our minds, we now need to go back and re-assess *that* moment when we share our faith with others. That moment seems so awkward, risky and costly that it's just not worth it. But compared to eternity, all of that changes.

Compared to eternity, the moment is no longer awkward, it is *urgent.* The sheer quantity of eternity immediately makes us realise that life is short, and it instantly confronts us with the reality that time is running out. That's why the New Testament urges us to make the best use of our time (Eph. 5:16, Col. 4:5). This is why Paul makes it so clear that what we believe needs to shape how we speak. If you go back to 2 Corinthians 4 and 5, Paul says that because we believe, we also speak (4:13). That speech has to be an open statement of truth (4:2), it is a proclamation of the lordship of Jesus (4:5). We will all appear before the judgement seat of Christ, so we persuade others (5:10-11). We are His ambassadors, imploring others to be reconciled to God (5:20).

All of that teaches us that the moment we share our faith with others is urgent. It is the most urgent need of every single person around us. And it also teaches us that, next to eternity, the 'safe' territory of not saying anything at all is actually a very dangerous place to go to. All around us, people are perishing. The outward body of every one of us is wasting away. Those moments when we speak to others about the hope we have in Jesus, are urgently, urgently needed.

Compared to eternity, the moment is not full of risk, it is full of *potential.* This is so crucial to recognise. The urgency of the moment is real, but if all we think about is the urgency, then it's likely that our motivation to speak will arise primarily from guilt. But we have better reasons to speak than guilt! The truth is, the moment that seems so risky is actually a moment that has such extraordinary potential. Think of all the people who Jesus spoke to: the woman at the well, the paralytic who was lowered through the roof, the woman who had been bleeding for years and years. They all had a moment which changed their lives forever. And the same is true for every believer. The moment when you met with Jesus has transformed everything. So, yes, the moment when you talk about Jesus with your friend might not be the easiest conversation you have ever had, it might be a bit strained, it might not be welcomed by them. But it might change their eternity. It might be a key link in the outworking of God's plan to bring that person from a path to death into a beautiful eternal relationship with Him. That is the amazing thing about how God works; even the tiniest moment can make a massive difference.

One of my favourite examples of this was when a friend of mine was talking about how he came to faith. His father had been very strict about church attendance growing up, but as an adult he had stopped going. This niggled at him, so one day he said to his wife, 'I think it would make my dad happy if I went to church.' My friend was nervous saying that because his wife didn't go to church at all. It was an awkward, risky, costly moment. But to his surprise she replied, 'I don't mind if we go to church.' As his wife watched on with tears in her eyes, my friend then said, 'That moment changed my life.' They both started attending church. They both came to faith in Jesus. Their eternities were transformed by a moment. Never forget that it only takes a moment for the

God, who said, 'Let light shine out of darkness,' to shine in our hearts in order to give the light of the knowledge of the glory of God in the face of Jesus Christ (see 2 Cor. 4:6).

Compared to eternity, the moment is not costly, it is *precious*. In 2 Corinthians 4, Paul gives a wonderful description of what we are like as we share the gospel. In verse 7, he tells us that we have treasure in jars of clay. That is teaching us that the moment when we share the gospel is not a moment we lose our reputation to our cost. It is a moment when we distribute the most valuable treasure that the world has ever known. And what makes it valuable is that it is treasure in heaven, it is treasure that lasts for eternity. So, in this life we all experience illness, injury and aging. In eternity with Jesus, there is full and total healing. Now, we experience the heartbreak of separation. In eternity with Jesus, there will be the beautiful reunion of all God's people. Now, we shed tears. In eternity with Jesus, they will be wiped away. Now, we experience pain and suffering. In eternity with Jesus, there will be joy that never fades. And best of all we will be with Him. As Paul says, 'he who raised the Lord Jesus will raise us also with Jesus and bring us with you into his presence' (2 Cor. 4:14). How precious is that?!

All of this means that, **when compared to eternity, the moment is definitely worth it**. That doesn't mean that the moment will be easy. It might be a light, momentary affliction. But may God write upon our hearts the fact that 'this light momentary affliction is preparing for us an eternal weight of glory beyond all comparison' (2 Cor. 4:17).

But as we speak, we must also make sure that 'we look not to the things that are seen but to the things that are unseen. For the things that are seen are transient, but the things that are unseen are eternal' (2 Cor. 4:18). That means that our perspective has got to look beyond the moment in front of us. The unseen reality of eternity is more important than the challenges of that moment when we share our faith, no matter how big those hurdles may look to us.

But I think this seen/unseen distinction is also important in relation to the person we are trying to talk to. So when you speak in that moment, you might see a hostile reaction. But underneath, there might be a desperate fear of death. You might see a blushing face. But underneath, there is a deep longing to know Jesus. You might see hesitation and swithering. But underneath, they wish more than anything that they had the same treasure as you. What we see and experience in the moment is not the whole story. The moment we are scared of might be the moment that they have been waiting for for years. You never know, maybe, in eternity, you will be sitting beside your friend recalling to them how terrified you were of the very moment that God used to lead them to eternal life through faith in Jesus. If you or I can be used by God to make a difference for eternity, then whatever that dreaded moment might bring, boy, it will be worth it.

The reality of eternity is inescapable. Knowing Jesus means that we have amazing treasure to share. It also means that we know how urgently needed our message is. We have something amazing to say and we have a massive reason to say it. We believe, therefore we will speak. The moment we do so might be hard, it might be awkward, and we will probably feel like we've done a bad job. None of that matters. God is infinite and eternal. He will fill in the gaps that our inadequacies will leave.

Tomorrow, there is a new opportunity for the moment to happen. That moment will probably be a bit scary. But never forget that a moment is just a moment. Eternity is what matters. And eternity is *eternity*.

STUDY QUESTIONS:

1. What things are you scared of? (Spiders, heights, snakes etc.)

2. What makes 'the moment' when you share your faith scary? In what ways is it awkward, risky and costly?

3. When you think of eternity, what do you think of?

4. Why do think Jesus defined eternal life as knowing the only true God and Jesus Christ whom He has sent? (John 17:3). What does that teach us about eternal life, both now and in the future?

5. How can thinking about eternity help encourage us to share our faith?

6. What might be unseen in the person that we are speaking to? How can focusing on these things help us?

PART TWO

YOU ARE YOU

CHAPTER SIX

You are You

〜〜

The first half of this book has been arguing that when it comes to sharing our faith, the most important truth we have to remember is that God is God. He is who He is. He is sovereign. He is able. He is willing. And on that basis we can look at any person, in any place, in any circumstances and know that the gospel we share with them can transform their lives. No matter who you look at, nothing is impossible because God is God.

That God reveals His truth to us, and that truth is the truth. Amazingly though, the truth He reveals is not a message of rejection. It is a gospel message, and that good news is good news. At the heart of the good news is His willingness to graciously give us what we never deserve; we are saved by grace. We never earn it, because grace is grace. That transforms our lives now and it gives us hope forevermore. The message that God reveals in Jesus is a message of eternal life. And nothing matters more than that, because eternity is eternity. All of these give us a firm foundation for sharing our faith. These are all theological truths that empower the work of evangelism.

But at this point, you may be very tempted to say, 'None of that is the problem. The problem is not God, or the truth He reveals, or the good news of the gospel, or the grace by which we are saved, or the eternity that awaits us. These are not the problem. The problem is *me*.'

God is God and He never changes, but if you are anything like me, then you will often look at yourself and wish that you were very different. I look at myself and I see a huge pile of weaknesses, failings and insecurities, all of which seriously undermine my efforts at evangelism. If that is how you feel then this chapter, and the rest of this book, is going to say something that you will probably find hard to believe. In terms of you sharing your faith, it is absolutely crucial that you must never, ever forget that you are you.

That might seem like a strange thing to say; it seems a bit obvious. But the fact that it is obvious means that it is all too easy to forget. If you think back to Chapter One, we saw that God appeared to Moses in a burning bush and called him to lead the people of Israel out of Egypt. In doing so, God gave a powerful revelation of Himself and left Moses in no doubt whatsoever that God is God. But at the very same time, Exodus 3 and 4 reveal that the God who is sovereign and powerful has chosen to work His purposes through a person who is very ordinary.

Right after God said to Moses, 'I AM WHO I AM,' He then tells Moses, 'Say this to the people of Israel, "I AM has sent me to you".' Moses is chosen by God to deliver His people out of Egypt. That must have been because he was so confident and talented, yes? Actually, no. If you read through Exodus 3 and 4 again, you discover that a big emphasis in the narrative is not that Moses is strong and capable, but that he is weak. Yet God comes to this weak, nervous, old shepherd in the middle of nowhere and He makes it very clear that He is going to use him. God is the great I AM. But the person He sends is a very ordinary 'me'. God took Moses as he was and He used him to do amazing things.

And this is where we see that **alongside the foundational truth that God is God lies the fact that you are you.** Why is this so important to remember for evangelism? Well, when it comes to sharing our faith with others, we can very often feel like evangelism is a work that is done by a select group of gifted experts, and we are definitely not one of them. We look at ourselves and see someone who doesn't know enough, who can't speak clearly enough and whose evangelistic zeal is drowned by a flood of fear and insecurity.

At the same time, we look at people who are good at evangelism and they seem so confident, so capable, so brave. They can talk to anyone, they have gone to all sorts of places, they've seen and done all sorts of things. And then we look back at ourselves and come to one of two conclusions. Either we think, 'I am not like that, therefore God cannot use me.' And we end up greatly discouraged and feeling pretty useless. Or we can think, 'I am not like that, so I need to become like that for God to use me.' The result is the idea that before God is going to use us, we need to undergo a fairly urgent personality transplant. And to achieve that, we try to change and copy other people who we see as far better at sharing their faith than we are. Or we just give up.

Now, it is absolutely the case that we can learn from others when it comes to sharing our faith. In fact, the New Testament encourages us to imitate those from whom we have heard the gospel. So this book is definitely not saying that when it comes to evangelising you can't and shouldn't learn from others.

But if you look at yourself and think that the biggest problem with your witnessing is you, if you think that witnessing is a job for others, or if you think that you need to undergo a radical personality overhaul in order to be used by God, then you are actually wrong. Very wrong. Theologically wrong. Because none of these conclusions are correct. When it comes to witnessing, you must not forget that God is God and you must never forget that you are you. Why is that?

First and foremost, the fact that you are you is simply the outworking of basic theological truths concerning the creation and providence of God. Think about these questions: Who formed you in your mother's womb? The biblical answer to that question is God. Who gave you the abilities you have? Again, the Bible says God. Whose image are you made in? God's. Who wrote the days of your life? God again. Who is ultimately responsible for your height, your hair colour, the sound of your voice, the pattern of your fingerprint? That would be God again. And over it all, who is your Creator? You know the answer. You see that so clearly in Exodus 4. Right after Moses laments how terrible he is at speaking, God replies by saying, 'Who has made man's mouth? Who makes him mute, or deaf, or seeing, or blind? Is it not I, the LORD?' (4:11).

So our theology tells us that the person we are, is a result of the work and plan of God. Now, that obviously does not include our sin. Sin is a rebellion against what God wants us to be and a horrible distortion of our God-created humanity. But in terms of our personality, our characteristics, our circumstances, we do not put these down simply to biological and sociological factors. We rightly regard these as the work of God.

So, if you go back to Exodus 3 and 4 and ask, who made Moses Moses? Who made him the meek, timid, not-very-keen-on-public-speaking Moses? The answer is that it was God. So who has made you *you*? It's the same answer: God. You are His workmanship. And that of course is why you are unique. It is why you are special. It is why you are not the same as anyone else. There are things about you that are the result of the deliberate plan of God. And that is also why you are not the useless piece of evangelistic hopelessness that you might think you are. You are you, and the person who did that is God. And that means that, just as God came to Moses as he was and where he was and used him for His glory, so too God can do exactly the same with you.

There are three specific things I'd like you to remember:

One: You are where you are

When we talk about God's providence, we are referring to the fact that we believe that God is in control of every detail of the universe and of our lives. He upholds, directs and governs all of His creation. So that means that our daily and weekly routine is part of what God has worked out in His wise and sovereign providence. So, let's apply this to evangelism: you are where you are. So, where are you going to be tomorrow? At home? At work? At school? In the community? At a friend's house? What will you be doing? Talking to people? Working? Attending to responsibilities? On social media?

Now ask the question: is any of what you are going to be doing tomorrow outside the providence of God? No. Absolutely none of it. So who has placed you where you are? God! And why do you think God has done that? It's because He has work there for you to do.

So in terms of sharing your faith, ask yourself the question, are you likely to have contact with an unbeliever tomorrow? Either in your home or at work or in your community or even at the supermarket. Are you going to interact with an unbeliever? If you are, which nearly all of us will be, then why do you think God's doing that? Why is the great work of ordering and sustaining the universe leading towards a convergence of you and an unbeliever tomorrow? Why is God doing that? It is because He can use people just like you. That's exactly why He opens up opportunities for us all the time.

Now that doesn't mean you are going to be able to have a gospel conversation at the supermarket checkout tomorrow. That kind of thing doesn't happen often. But it does mean that where you are right now is a massive opportunity for you to be a light in this world. Your prayers for the people you know might be the only time that anyone mentions that person to God. Your speech, your conduct, your interest in others, your acts of kindness, your

83

self-control, all of these things can be an immensely powerful witness to the people you meet. And alongside that constant witness of our behaviour, God can open up opportunities for you to tell someone that Jesus has made a massive difference to your life. That can happen in a car, on a walk, in a café, across the desk at work, anywhere. You are where you are. And if God is God, then He can definitely use you there.

Two: You are who you are

Every single Christian is different. We all have different personalities, different strengths, different weaknesses, different fears. But the great thing about God is that He uses all sorts of different people in order to spread the good news of Jesus. In the Bible, you have the quiet Moses, the bold (and sometimes depressed) Elijah, the over-enthusiastic Peter, the grafting Martha, the contemplating Mary, the fearless Stephen, the persuasive Paul, the nervous Timothy.

And throughout history, it has been the same. You have the blunt Martin Luther, the studious John Calvin, the conflict-averse Philip Melanchthon, the devoted-but-most-of-the-time-unwell Robert Murray M'Cheyne, and the apparently-not-smart-enough Gladys Aylward. God has used thousands of very different people through whom He has done amazing work.

Central to this is the wonderful teaching that the Bible gives us regarding the gifts of the Holy Spirit. All Christians have certain gifts from God the Holy Spirit: some have some, some have others, no one has all, and no one has none. Some have a gift of evangelism, and that is why, from time to time, we do meet people who are very natural and capable evangelists. But at no point does the New Testament say that only those with the gift of evangelism should spread the gospel. The command to make disciples is given to all disciples. And that means that you, with the gifts that you have, can be used by God too. But how do you know where your gifts lie?

Well, there's lots that could be said about discerning gifts, but sometimes the most helpful things are the most obvious of all. Step one for discovering what gifts you have is to ask: what do you actually like doing? Yes, you read that correctly, what do you like doing? Because the things that you really like doing are very likely to be the areas where you have a gift through which God can use you to share the gospel.

So if you like meeting people, then go for it: make friends, go for coffees, have people for dinner and build up a relationship with them whereby they can see that you have something wonderful in your life. If you like organising things, then go for it: get stuck in to help with church and community events. If you like helping people, then just go for it: help people either through visiting them, or sending them a card or a text or by offering to give them a hand with something. If you like being generous and are able to, then keep being generous and look for new opportunities, big or small, to do so. If you like sport, then get involved with sport in your community. Same with art, music, drama, whatever your interest may be. If you like teaching, then pray for opportunities to teach others, either one to one or in a small group. Whatever it is, very often what we like doing can be a great avenue for serving God and sharing your faith.

And this raises a really important point about evangelism, which possibly goes against a phrase that you may have often heard said in church or among Christians. When it comes to evangelising, and indeed many aspects of our lives as disciples, we are frequently told that we need to 'get out of our comfort zone'. Now, that is a helpful phrase if it's a reminder that laziness is not appropriate in the life of a Christian. But there is a danger that the call to 'get out of our comfort zone' is implying that if we are going to be used by God, we have to be doing something that we are utterly terrified of. But it doesn't always have to be like that. In fact, the gifts that God has given you mean that there will be areas of life where you feel more confident, more capable, in fact more comfortable, and these are the areas where God can do amazing things through you.

So if you are lazy, then yes, definitely get out of your comfort zone. But if you are longing to share your faith but you feel crippled by nerves, then you don't need to get out of your comfort zone; you need to maximise your comfort zone. In other words, you need to think about the things you love doing, the areas where you feel most confident and comfortable, and then maximise what you can do through them for the glory of God. Now obviously that does not mean something sinful; that should go without saying. But whatever it is that you love doing, just think, pray and plan how that might become an opportunity for you to reach out to people who need to hear the gospel. Sometimes, our frustration and disappointment about what we *lack* can cause us to miss the enormous opportunities that are presented through what we *like*.

Three: You are how you are

One of the many amazing things about the Bible is that it is utterly realistic. It never pretends that Christians are superwomen or supermen, nor does it ever suggest that the Christian life is a bed of roses. The Bible recognises the struggles and battles of life, and it speaks candidly about the fragility of people like you.

But when it comes to sharing our faith, surely we want to show people that everything is wonderful? Surely we want to give the impression that following Jesus has made everything brilliant in our lives? And, if we are struggling, surely we want to hide that and make sure that we put on a good outward face? Well, not necessarily.

When it comes to sharing your faith, you are where you are, you are who you are, but you are also *how* you are. And how you are might be very different at different times. So, yes, there are times as Christians when we do feel amazing and sometimes these are the times when we feel most like sharing our faith. And that out-pouring of enthusiasm can be very helpful, although it can also run the risk of being a bit annoying!

But often we don't feel amazing as Christians. We get tired, we face disappointments, we worry about things, and we get hurt and bruised by life. Can we evangelise when we feel like that? Is evangelism like football where, if you are injured, you stay on the side-lines until you are fully fit again? No, I don't think it is. Sharing our faith is something we can do no matter how we are feeling.

In fact, honesty about how we are feeling can actually be a hugely powerful element of our evangelism. Saying to someone, 'My life is great because I am a Christian' can actually be more off-putting than it is appealing. And if it's not true, then it is another example of hypocrisy. But saying to someone, 'I have had a hard week, but my faith in Jesus gives me strength and hope that makes a real difference' can show someone who has the same struggles that Jesus might just be what they need more than anything else.

When you share your faith, you are how you are. In other words, our evangelism must display integrity. Our best evangelism is not when we are putting on a show, or trying to impress, or conforming to a type. Our best evangelism is when, by the grace and power of Jesus Christ working in us, we are being ourselves. That's why it's so important to remember that you are you.

You are not ...

The fact that you are you, however, also means that there are certain things that you are not. And this is where being part of a church is such a blessing. As you try to reach out to others, if you come up against something that you are not good at, you have an army of fellow workers in the church who can help you. So if someone asks you a question you can't answer, don't panic. Tell them that you've got a friend at church who could probably help. If you can't cope with finances, then there are people at church who can. If you are not very good at cooking or hosting people, there are people at church who can help.

The key point is that you can use the gifts you have for the glory of God, and your brothers and sisters in the church can help you when it comes to the gifts that you don't have, or with the gifts that are only just beginning to flicker into flame in your life. And again, we can see that with Moses. In Exodus 4, Moses tells God, 'I am not an eloquent speaker, can't you send someone else?' In reply, God says, with marvellous simplicity, 'That's not a problem, your brother Aaron can speak, so he's coming with you.'

The crucial thing to remember is that you – you *where* you are, *who* you are and *how* you are, you with the personality and gifts you have – you can be used by God. That is not optimistic niceness to make you feel better. It is a rock solid theological fact. And when we recognise that, it should give us a much greater sense of readiness and excitement each day. We want to get up every morning and pray that today would be a day where our gifts would be used by God. So we can pray that we would be led to the person who needs encouragement. We can pray that we would be able to welcome the person who is lonely into our home. We can pray that our administration would honour God in a clear and obvious way. We can pray that our words would help point people to Jesus. We can pray that our conduct would show everyone around us that we have something so special in our lives.

You are you. That means you have a unique set of contacts and circumstances and gifts for sharing the gospel, and the fact that God is God means that He is more than capable of using all these things for His glory. So is tomorrow an exciting day for the gospel? Too right it is! If God is God, then He absolutely can use someone like you. In fact, He can use the person who actually is *you*.

STUDY QUESTIONS:

1. When you think of sharing your faith, in what ways do you wish you were different? Are all these appropriate?

2. Think of the different people God used in the Bible. Who do you feel most like? In what ways?

3. Think of the people that God used in your own journey to faith. Were they all the same or were they different? In what ways? How did God use them?

4. Think about *where*, *who* and *how* you are. How are each of these important when it comes to sharing your faith?

5. In what ways could you 'maximise your comfort zone' in order to reach out to others?

6. If you are in a small group, what gifts do you see in the people around you that they could maximise for sharing their faith? How can you help and encourage each other to do this?

CHAPTER SEVEN

Witnessing is Witnessing

Every so often in life, we have those moments when something is shown to us that we had never realised but, once it has been pointed out, seems so obvious that we find ourselves thinking, 'How on earth did I not see this before?' One of my favourite examples of this is a friend of mine who came back from a summer camp saying, 'I only just found out that Banoffee Pie is called "Banoffee" because it has got banana and toffee in it!' Prior to this discovery, he had always thought that 'Banoffee' was just a random name. It has happened to me lots of times as well. I only recently discovered that 'Pokémon' is called that because it is short for 'Pocket Monster'. Likewise, who knew that the word 'fortnight' is short for fourteen nights? I didn't, for the first thirty-nine years of my life! More embarrassingly, I was again well into my thirties when I realised that when the UK Parliament announces the result of a vote in the House of Commons, when the tellers shout out, 'The eyes to the right ... the nose to the left ...' they aren't talking about parts of your face. It is, of course, 'Aye's' and 'No's' rather than 'eyes' and 'nose', which is so obvious that I really do worry that it took me over thirty years to realise it!

I had one of those moments when I read Rico Tice's brilliant little book, *Honest Evangelism*. This is the paragraph I read:

> Our job is not to convert people. It is to witness to Christ. Conversion isn't the mark of successful witness – witnessing is. Think of a courtroom. Witnesses are there to tell the truth. That's successful witness. If the jury doesn't believe them, that's not their fault or their failure. You have not failed if you explain the gospel and are rejected. You have failed if you don't try.[1]

When I read those words I discovered something incredibly obvious but which I had never seen before. I realised that the task of witnessing is not to convert someone. The task of witnessing is to be a witness. It is to testify to the truth of who Jesus is and what He has done. This was one of the biggest light bulb moments in my Christian life. For years, whenever I had thought of witnessing, I had always reasoned that if it didn't result in a conversion, then it was a failure (which was why I felt like such a poor witness myself). But Rico Tice showed me what I had never seen before, but which now seems so obvious. Witnessing isn't converting someone. That, of course, makes perfect sense because converting someone is something only God can do. It is not the witness's job. The witness's job is to be a witness. That's why, when it comes to sharing our faith, we have got to remember that witnessing is *witnessing*.

From the beginning of the New Testament Church, witnessing has been a key part of what Jesus wants and needs His people to do. In Acts 1, just before He ascended into heaven, Jesus told His disciples:

> … you will receive power when the Holy Spirit has come upon you, and you will be my witnesses in Jerusalem and in all Judea and Samaria, and to the end of the earth (Acts 1:8).

The rest of Acts tells of how that work of witnessing began, from the events of Pentecost in Jerusalem in chapter 2, all the way through

---

1. Rico Tice, *Honest Evangelism* (Epsom: The Good Book Company, 2015), 56.

to Paul's arrival in Rome in chapter 28. Central to that witness was the reality of Jesus' resurrection. The Apostles had met with the risen Jesus Himself (which was a key aspect of what qualified them to be apostles) and they testified to what they had seen with their own eyes. But in the generations since, even though we are not eye-witnesses of resurrection appearances in the way that the Apostles were, nevertheless every Christian is called to bear witness to the reality of Jesus' resurrection and the transforming power that He has brought into our lives. In fact, this is the last thing that Jesus said to His Church before ascending into heaven: 'You will be *my* witnesses.' That *you* includes me, and it includes you.

Witnessing: What is it?

Witnessing is part of the job description of every Christian. But that immediately raises two big problems for all of us. The first is that none of us feel up to the job. If you are anything like me, then you will be in a constant battle against the feeling that you are totally inadequate for the task. But it is important to remember those kinds of feelings are actually the norm, not the exception. Moses, Elijah, Jeremiah, Peter, Paul, Timothy and countless others are way ahead of you in the queue of Christians who know that, without Jesus' help, we cannot do anything. But the second problem is more subtle and probably more dangerous. Our problem is not just that we don't feel up to the job. Our problem is that all too often, we give ourselves the wrong job.

Let me explain what I mean. Rico Tice tells us to think of a courtroom, so imagine one in your minds. In that courtroom there are several jobs. Our problem is that, when it comes to sharing our faith, we can easily fall into the trap of picking a job that's not ours to take.

So, sometimes, we can think our job is to be the **Prosecution**. We see someone who isn't a Christian and we try to confront them with the reality of their sin; we interrogate them concerning all that is wrong in their lives; we expose their guilt and failings; we might even threaten them with the reality of hell.

Sometimes, we can think of ourselves as the **Defence**. So we fight back if we feel that Christianity is being threatened; we are confrontational towards people who think differently; we are defensive if questions are asked that we might not be able to answer.

Sometimes, we can think of ourselves as the **Press**. So we keep a close eye on what's happening in someone's life; we are quick to make a noise if something scandalous happens; we are keen to talk more about people than we are to talk to people.

Sometimes, we can even think of ourselves as the **Judge**. So we cast our verdict on people, on their circumstances, on their mistakes.

And sometimes, perhaps even most of the time, we can think that our job is just to sit in the public gallery. We are onlookers in this work of evangelism, keen to see what happens, but not so keen to actually be involved.

Now, in saying all that, I am not denying the fact that in sharing the gospel there are times when we have to try to get people to recognise the reality of sin; we do need to be ready to defend our faith and give a reason for the hope that is in us; we may need to make appropriate judgements; we must try and learn about what is actually going on in people's lives, and there will be times when looking on in silence is wise. But what we must recognise is that the primary task that Jesus has given us is not to be the Prosecution, the Defence, the Judge, the Press or the Public watching on. Your primary task is to be the *witness*.

And the crucial point we need to recognise is that the key thing that a witness does is this: they talk about someone else. Their job is to bear witness to the truth that they know about someone else. And this is why the little word 'my' in Acts 1:8 is so important; Jesus said, 'You will be *my* witnesses.' Our primary job is not to prosecute, defend, judge, report or watch. Witnessing is none of those things. Witnessing is *witnessing*. Our job is to testify about *Him*. We bear witness to the truth that we have discovered about Jesus Christ.

This is where we find another truth that is so obvious, yet so easy to miss. When it comes to witnessing, we must remember that talking about Jesus is talking about *Jesus*. I say that because it is something that I have got wrong so many times. So often, when I try to share my faith, I end up speaking about things like church services, or church attendance, or about issues facing the church. Or I talk about people connected to the church, locally or nationally. Sometimes I might talk about something I have read, or maybe even about a Christian from history. None of that is wrong; these are all good things to talk about. But none of that 'talking about Jesus' is actually talking about Jesus. And yet that is what lies at the heart of what witnessing is all about. To be His witnesses, we need to be talking about Him!

So, we need to talk about who He is: how He is the most captivating person in all of history, how He is so full of wisdom, compassion and grace, how He is so worthy of all our worship, how He is the best friend that we could ever have, how He fills the gap in our lives that nothing else can satisfy. And we need to talk about what He has done: how He welcomed outcasts, how He challenged injustice, how He came not to be served but to serve, how He healed the broken, taught the confused, washed the feet of His disciples, ate and drank with sinners, laid down His life to save us. The most amazing thing we can ever talk about is *Him*! That's what we want our testimony to be. That is what we want to talk about. Witnessing is telling people what we know about Jesus. It is telling them about how outstanding He is and about the amazing difference that He has made to our lives. Witnessing isn't about skirting around the numerous topics vaguely connected to Jesus. Witnessing is showing and telling our family, friends and neighbours the truth, the whole truth and nothing but the truth …

about Him! The success of our witnessing is not determined by whether or not we see a conversion in the person standing in front of us. The success of our witnessing is determined by whether or not the person standing in front of us sees more of Jesus in the person who is standing in front of them.

Witnessing: Who does it?

The question of 'Who?' in regard to witnessing is also one that we can easily get wrong. On the one hand, sharing our faith can very often feel like a very lonely experience. When we think about doing it, we feel like everyone else is better at it than us. When we do it, we feel very exposed and vulnerable. Once we've done it, we can be left riddled with frustration at everything we wish we had said and done better. When it comes to witnessing, it is very easy to feel isolated and alone. On the other hand, it is so easy to feel excluded. There may be many good witnesses out there, but I am not one of them. When it comes to the 'Who?' of witnessing, it is so easy to conclude that it is either me on my own, or it is everyone else doing it without me.

Neither of these conclusions are theologically correct. If we look again at Acts 1:8, we discover the amazing truth that witnessing is something we all do together. When Jesus said, 'You will be my witnesses,' the 'you' and the 'witnesses' are plural. That means that, when Jesus commissioned the church to bear witness about Him, He didn't send out a crowd of individuals, He sent out a team. We are all members of that team. And what an incredible team it is!

Let's start with the founding members. Now, in terms of founding members, you might immediately think of Peter, James, John and the other Apostles who Jesus speaks to in Acts 1. Surely these men are the founding members of Jesus' team of witnesses? Well, actually no. The founding members of the team witnessing for Jesus are God the Father, God the Son and God the Holy Spirit.

In terms of witnessing, it is the triune God Himself who leads the way. In John 8:18, Jesus said, 'I am the one who bears witness about myself, and the Father who sent me bears witness about me.' Then, in John 15:26, Jesus says that 'when the Helper comes, whom I will send to you from the Father, the Spirit of truth, who proceeds from the Father, he will bear witness about me.' The first and primary witnesses to the truth about Jesus are God the Father, Jesus Himself as God the Son, and God the Holy Spirit. And that means that in all our work of witnessing, we are just continuing a work that God Himself has already begun.

From that glorious starting point, the witnessing team of Jesus grows and grows. The Apostles were added, going from place to place sharing the good news. They were joined by others, so soon you had Paul and Barnabas, Silas and Timothy, Priscilla and Aquila, and many, many more. This has continued down through the centuries: thousands and thousands of ordinary people called by God to join His team of witnesses. And the amazing thing is that God has placed you in that team as well. This is the crucial point: you are not a supporter of the team; you are not on the side-lines of the team, you are a member! That means that when Jesus calls you to be His witness, He is calling you to be part of something incredible. God the Father, God the Son and God the Holy Spirit began a work of witnessing. Today, God has placed you on His team to continue that work. That is such an incredible privilege, and such an exciting opportunity!

Some of you may be fans of rock music. If so, you will know many of the biggest rock bands in the world: U2, the Rolling Stones, Led Zepplin, the Eagles. But none of these is the greatest rock band of all. The greatest rock band of all is Runrig. Now, anyone not from Scotland will be saying, 'Who??!' Well, let me tell you. Runrig were a Celtic rock group from Scotland whose career lasted over forty-five years, until they finally retired in 2018. They may not be known worldwide, but they could sell out Scotland's biggest venues in minutes. (If you have never heard them, get on Spotify and have a listen!) For their final eighteen years, their keyboard player was a man called Brian Hurren. And the story of how he joined the band is brilliant.

He was aged twenty and nearing the end of his music studies when one of his lecturers told him that a band were auditioning for a keyboard player and he thought Brian should try. While rehearsing for the audition, the band's manager phoned him and during the conversation Brian asked, 'Is it just Runrig songs that this band plays?' It was at that moment when he realised that he wasn't being asked to audition for a Runrig cover band. He was auditioning for the real thing! The rest, as they say, is history; the audition went well and for the next eighteen years Brian was a member of the greatest rock band the world has ever (or perhaps not yet?!) known.

Why am I telling you that story? I am telling it to you because Brian did not realise that he was being asked to be part of something phenomenal. All too often, we are the same. We can so easily think that there's no room for us in Jesus' team of witnesses. It's so easy to think that we just aren't at that level. But that is not true. You are on the team. You are part of something incredible.

And that is why in your witnessing, you don't have to do it all. You don't need to explain every detail of the gospel. You don't need to bring someone from unbelief to regeneration in the space of a ten-minute conversation. You don't need to have an answer to every question. You just need to share what you know about Jesus. In doing so, you might be a very small link in a very big chain that God is using to bring that person to faith in Jesus. Never forget that it is very rare for God to use one single witness alone in someone's journey to faith. He will use other people to fill in the areas that you weren't able to cover. When it comes to witnessing, you are not isolated, and you are not excluded. You are part of an amazing team.

Witnessing: When does it happen?

But it is not just the 'Who?' question that we can easily get wrong. The same danger applies to the question of 'When?' So when does witnessing happen? Well, if I look at my own life, my instinctive answer to that question is, 'Not very often.' The conversations that we long to have with our friends feel very rare. Opportunities to share the gospel don't come around very often. For that reason, we might pray that we would be a witness in our lives, and in praying that prayer, our hope is: a) that a moment might arise when we can share our faith with someone and b) that when it does arrive, we won't make a complete hash of it. And that is a good prayer to pray. We want opportunities to arise, and we definitely want to be ready for the moment when they do. But if we think that the 'When?' of witnessing is confined to those moments when a conversation about the gospel takes place, then we are totally wrong.

So when does witnessing happen? The answer is that it happens from the moment you come to faith in Jesus right through to the moment when He takes you home to heaven at the end of your life, and there is never a single second in between when you are not doing it. Witnessing, in other words, is a constant activity in the life of every Christian. When we come to faith, we join His team of witnesses, and we stay on that team for the rest of our lives.

The implications of this are enormous. It tells us that witnessing is not something that we sometimes do and sometimes don't do. Witnessing is something that we constantly do, but sometimes we do it well and sometimes we do it badly. So yes, there are times when we will speak specifically about the good news of Jesus with people around us. But these moments are occasional. Alongside them is the fact that twenty-four hours a day, seven days a week, the way you behave is saying something about Jesus to everyone who can see you.

This explains why Jesus, and the whole New Testament, places such a strong emphasis on good works in the lives of Christians. A great example is in Matthew 5. Here, Jesus teaches about witnessing. He tells His disciples that they are the light of the world, and in explaining how that witnessing works, Jesus says, 'Let your light shine before others, so that they may see your good works and give glory to your Father who is in heaven' (Matt. 5:16). That verse tells us that the good works in the lives of Christians are a constant witness bearing testimony to the transformation that the risen Jesus has brought in our lives. But likewise, bad behaviour in the life of a Christian massively undermines the witness that we bear. That's part of the reason why, later in the New Testament, James says that faith without works is useless and dead (James 2:17-20).

It is easy to think that witnessing is a bit like exercise. It is something everyone should do, something that we sometimes do, something that some people do much more than others, but for everyone it is still only occasional. Witnessing is not like that. Witnessing is actually like breathing; we do it all the time, whether we realise it or not, and sometimes we do it more intensely when the need arises. That is what witnessing is like. There are times when we will have opportunities to speak about Jesus, and these moments are an enormous privilege. In those moments, we will breathe harder as we seek to share the truth about who Jesus is and about the amazing difference He has made to our lives. But when those moments pass, the witnessing doesn't stop. The breathing goes on as our day-to-day conduct, speech, reactions, attitudes, generosity and, above all, our love for God and for others bears constant witness to our Saviour. And the importance of that constant day-to-day witness of our good works cannot be understated. If that constant witness is strong, then it will back up everything we try to say on the occasions when we do get to talk to someone about Jesus. But if the constant witness of our behaviour is poor, then when we eventually do try to share our faith with others, we have already undermined everything that we are hoping to say to them.

There's one other situation that we need to think about in terms of 'When?' This is a subject that Jesus identifies as a particularly powerful opportunity for witnessing. In fact, there is a strong case to say that this one topic is the single most effective moment for witnessing to take place. This is arguably the situation that God uses more than any other. This brings witnessing opportunities that are on another level altogether. What is it? It's persecution.

In Luke 21, Jesus prophesies to His disciples about what the future experience of the church will be, particularly in the decades following Jesus' ascension, although the implications of what He says continue on until He returns. He says to His disciples, 'There will be great earthquakes, and in various places famines and pestilences. And there will be terrors and great signs from heaven. But before all this they will lay their hands on you and persecute you, delivering you up to the synagogues and prisons, and you will be brought before kings and governors for my name's sake. *This will be your opportunity to bear witness'* (Luke 21:11-13).

And throughout the whole history of the Christian church, Jesus' words have been proved true again and again. It is in moments of suffering that the witness of Christians has been the most powerful. Sometimes, that suffering was unimaginable. Sometimes, it cost people their lives. Our English word 'martyr' comes from the Greek word that simply means 'witness'. But in the midst of suffering and persecution, the witness of ordinary believers has been incredibly powerful. That, of course, explains why the Apostles didn't pray for persecution to be taken away. They prayed that, in the midst of persecution, Christians would remain faithful in their witness. Often, we think that persecution is a bad sign, and we pray that it would go away. But if what Jesus says is true, that means that if we pray for persecution to go away, we might very well be in danger of praying away the greatest witnessing opportunities that we could ever have.

So, witnessing is witnessing. It happens constantly through our day-to-day behaviour, it happens occasionally when we have opportunity to speak about Jesus, and it happens with particular power when the church of Jesus Christ is attacked. It's a work that we do together, as one great team. And it is all about sharing the truth that we have discovered about Jesus and the power of His resurrection. But having said all that, if you still feel weak, inadequate or incapable for the task, then there's one final piece of the witnessing jigsaw that you will find in Acts 1:8. Jesus said, 'You will receive *power* ... and you will be my witnesses.' Your work as a witness for Jesus is empowered by Jesus through God the Holy Spirit. That means that, as you witness, you are not just talking about Jesus' power, you are talking *with* Jesus' power.

On Sundays, I have often prayed that I would be a witness in the week ahead, and in my mind, I am thinking in terms of having opportunities to witness at certain points in the week. I have come to realise that is not the precise prayer I need to pray. I don't need to pray to be a witness, because I am already a witness and I don't actually have a choice in the matter. In Acts 1:8, Jesus didn't make not being a witness an option. So what I need to pray is not that I would be a witness. I need to pray that I would be a *credible* witness. We need to pray that our witnessing would be so genuine, so consistent and so convincing that it is impossible for the people around us to ignore.

STUDY QUESTIONS:

1. In terms of witnessing, in what ways do you feel weak or inadequate?

2. Think about the courtroom image again. Can you think of examples of how we are prone to take a job that isn't ours?

3. 'Talking about Jesus is talking about Jesus.' How can we ensure that Jesus, and not simply subjects loosely connected to Him, is the main subject we speak about?

4. In what ways does being part of a team of witnesses encourage you?

5. Why is our behaviour so important in terms of our witness? What patterns of behaviour risk undermining the credibility of our witness, both as individuals and as a congregation?

6. How do you feel about the thought of experiencing persecution?

CHAPTER EIGHT

Evil is Evil

◇◇◇

Among the many objections to Christianity that have appeared over the centuries, one of the most common is known as the problem of evil. The argument goes something along the lines of, 'If there is a God, why is there so much suffering in the world?' Perhaps the most famous advocate of this argument was the eighteenth-century Scottish philosopher David Hume. He reasoned that the existence of a good and powerful God cannot be compatible with the reality of evil. If God can't stop evil, He can't be powerful. If God won't stop evil, He can't be good. And many others have made the same kind of argument over the years.

How do we answer this problem? Well, first of all it is worth noting that, without God, we have an even bigger problem trying to explain what makes something good in the first place. But secondly, it is important to see that the solution doesn't actually lie in the question of who God is or in what He can or cannot do. The answer lies in the question of who we are. And in regard to that, the Bible teaches us that we have been created with an extraordinary dignity which places us in a position of unique privilege and unique responsibility. A key aspect of that dignity was freedom, which is simultaneously a wonderful privilege and a solemn responsibility. Anyone who has let a toddler climb the stairs for the first time will know that the moment freedom is granted, it creates wonderful opportunities to thrive, and at the very same time it introduces the all-too-real risk of falling.

It is our failure to use that freedom wisely that has resulted in a broken world. Humanity rebelled, sinned and fell from the place God created for us to enjoy. That's not a reality we find easy to accept, especially today. In the individualistic mindset that shapes the society around us, we like to isolate ourselves from personal blame and corporate responsibility. David Hume wanted to make the problem of evil God's problem, not ours. But in doing so, we are simply trying (yet again) to mask the fact that the sin and suffering in the world is a consequence of our actions. In fact, it's actually quite ironic that the David Humes of this world want to be free enough to judge God while simultaneously claiming that we aren't free enough to be held responsible for ignoring Him. You don't need to be a philosopher to see that that makes no sense. The truth is, we have abused the privilege of freedom, we have no one to blame but ourselves.

Still, for many people, when it comes to Christianity, thinking about evil is a problem. However, when it comes to sharing the good news of the gospel, thinking about evil is actually immensely helpful. In fact, rather than being a stumbling block, thinking about evil can be a goldmine of encouragement as we seek to tell others about Jesus. But in order for it to help us, we have got to recognise that evil is *evil*.

Understanding evil

At first glance, to say that evil is evil is not controversial. You will struggle to find someone who disagrees, no matter what they believe. But if we think about it a little bit more, we discover that although we might all say that evil is evil, the way we live our lives says something very different. Here are three examples of how this happens.

One: Today, evil is acceptable. That doesn't apply to all forms of evil; thankfully, many terrible wrongs are still called out and held to account. But many evils are accepted. That happens in two main ways. On the one hand, societies can endorse actions that are morally indefensible. The rise of abortion is perhaps the most tragic example of this in recent history. As Paul rightly observed in Romans 1, people not only do things that are wrong; they also give approval to those who do them (Rom. 1:32). But, on the other hand (and this is the one that we are probably much more in danger of doing), we can so easily resign ourselves to the evil around us to the point where something horrendous just doesn't bother us very much. So we see high drug deaths as inevitable: when dozens of people are killed in a terrorist attack in Central Asia or sub-Saharan Africa, it is never as big a headline as who won the Oscars. Even in the church, we have long since grown numb to the horrific reality of a divided Christian family. All of this is a long way from Paul's instruction in Romans 12:9, to 'abhor what is evil; hold fast to what is good'.

Two: Today, evil is entertaining. This can be evidenced in a thousand ways. Books, newspapers, TV shows, movies, internet – all of these provide a feast of entertainment which glamorises behaviour that is appalling. That doesn't mean to say that the arts must never portray the reality of sin. Even the Bible does that; the wisdom literature of the Old Testament, for instance, describes many things that are evil in order to make a point. But we've long since gone past the point of appropriate presentation of the immoral in order to express an important reality. We've made the immoral a fantasy that we cannot get enough of. But it is not just the arts and the internet that find evil entertaining. So often our conversations follow the same path. In Romans 1:29-30, Paul lists gossip, slander and boasting among the debased activities that ought not to be done. Yet we so frequently delight in a bit of scandal, we make jokes at the expense of others, and we love to think that we are just that wee bit better than the people around us whom we're talking about.

Three, and most worryingly of all: Today, evil is useful. Deceit can take you to the very top in politics. Exploitation of a labour force can make you very rich. Disclosing private information about someone can give you a lot of power. Many people suffer because they are on the receiving end of evil behaviour that is being used by people as a means of getting what they want.

Over against all of this, the Bible tells us that evil is evil. It is not acceptable, it is not entertaining, and it absolutely must not be used to accomplish anything. It is hideous. This is where we need to realise that the abhorrence for evil which the Bible expects is not the fun-spoiling demand of boring religious fanaticism. It is the recognition that evil is absolutely horrible. It is the plea that we accurately understand and steadfastly avoid the behaviour that wrecks precious individuals, destroys our communities and devastates humanity.

This is a fascinating thing to think about, because this whole topic is an area where people seem to make very big, and sometimes quite bizarre, misjudgements about Christianity. Everyone knows that there are certain things that the Bible regards as evil, but if you ask the question, 'What kind of behaviour do people think is most offensive to God?' there seem to be some astonishing misunderstandings about the answer. You discover these when you look out for the things that people apologise for when they find out that you are a Christian.

The one I've come across most is swearing (and by that I mean bad language, not blasphemy). Many times, people have sworn in front of me and then frantically apologised when they realised that I am a Christian. Another is church attendance. People often apologise for either missing church or for not attending at all. And the most bizarre one of all is children; people will apologise if young children make too much noise in a church service or activity.

Now, it is absolutely true that swearing is not a good habit. Likewise, church attendance is definitely important. The children one, however, is ridiculous because God utterly delights in welcoming little ones. But the key point is that this is the stuff that people apologise for. But is that really the stuff that bothers God the most? Are these the areas where He demands an apology? Is this the behaviour that should horrify Christians?

Not according to the Bible. Anyone who thinks that these are the things God is concerned about is totally misunderstanding what God considers to be evil. Scripture shows us the issues that really bother God. There are many, here are just some examples:

Injustice. Again and again in the Old Testament, God was angered by the cruelty and neglect shown towards the vulnerable. In Isaiah 1, God says that He is absolutely fed up with the nation's religious observance because, while they made a show of their acts of piety, they were corrupt and they failed to help the widows and fatherless (see Isa. 1:11-23). Today, the world is still full of injustice. To the God whose commitment to justice is utterly impeccable, it is a great evil.

Deceit. Psalm 34:13 says 'Keep your tongue from evil and your lips from speaking deceit.' James describes the tongue as 'a restless evil, full of deadly poison' (James 3:8). The Bible never underestimates the potential for harm that can come through deception. It is a reminder that our words, whether spoken, written or typed, can easily be inaccurate, can all too often be dishonest, and are therefore highly likely to be very damaging. Today, we are swamped with half-truths, fake news, spin and manipulation. To the God whose adherence to the truth is absolute, that deception is a serious evil.

Abuse. The Bible frequently uses the image of a shepherd to describe those in positions of leadership. Sometimes the image speaks positively, like when describing David, Old Testament Israel's greatest King (see 2 Sam. 5:2 and 7:7). But sometimes, the imagery is used to give a sharp rebuke to Israel's leadership. Jeremiah does this in chapter 23 of his prophecy:

> 'Woe to the shepherds who destroy and scatter the sheep of my pasture!' declares the LORD. Therefore thus says the LORD, the God of Israel, concerning the shepherds who care for my people: 'You have scattered my flock and have driven them away, and you have not attended to them. Behold, I will attend to you for your evil deeds, declares the LORD' (Jer. 23:1-2).

Ezekiel 34 does the same. In the Old Testament, leaders failed because they mistreated the people who depended on them. Today, little has changed. Power is used to abuse others in homes, in workplaces, in businesses, in nations, and even in churches. To God, in whom infinite, eternal and unchangeable power is never divorced from infinite, eternal and unchangeable goodness, when people use power and authority to abuse those who are under their care, it is a hideous evil.

Revenge. This is the one occasion when evil seems to be more acceptable, when we've been on the receiving end of evil ourselves it seems fair to do the same back. So, if someone lies to us, we think it OK to lie in return. If someone hurts us, we are glad to see them get hurt too. If someone treats us unfairly, it can actually feel quite good to do the same back to them. But Romans 12 tells us that responding to evil with more of the same is not good at all. It is evil. Paul says in verse 17, 'Repay no one evil for evil.' That's teaching us that evil provoked by evil is still evil. It's a solemn reminder that we must never use sin as an excuse for more sin. We must do the exact opposite. As Paul tells us in Romans 12:21, we must overcome evil, not with more evil, but with good. Peter says exactly the same thing (1 Pet. 3:9). Both of them are simply repeating what Jesus taught in the Sermon on the Mount (Matt. 5:38-48).

All these show us that in God's eyes evil is not acceptable, it is never entertaining and it must not be used. Evil is to be abhorred.

It is unfair, because it is a tool for dishing out injustice to people. It is wrong, because it deceives people with lies. It is dangerous, because it leaves people bruised and scarred. And it is toxic; left unchecked, it will poison and pollute our lives. Evil is evil.

Evil and sharing the gospel

But what does all that have to do with helping us share our faith? Well, it can actually be incredibly helpful because it presses home to us two key truths that lie at the heart of why we want to tell other people about Jesus.

First, recognising that evil is evil reminds us of *why the gospel is urgently needed.* If we look back at our own lives, we quickly discover that when it comes to evil, it is both something that we do and it is something that is done to us. So sometimes, we are the ones whose behaviour is wrong. Our thoughts, our speech, our actions are all potential channels for evil to flow through. One of the most sobering experiences we can have is when we realise just what a human being is capable of. But equally, we can be on the receiving end of evil behaviour, and every one of us knows first-hand how hard that is. And all around us, people are being battered physically, emotionally and spiritually by the ruthless reality of evil. All of this means that we can cheat and get cheated, deceive and get deceived, hurt and get hurt. And that's why it's not the case that some people are good and some people are evil. The truth is, we are all a mixture of both. We are humans, made by God to bear His image. But we are also sinners, marred by corruption. When it comes to evil, we are all too capable, and we are very, very vulnerable.

We desperately need deliverance from both of these realities. And the people you live with, work with, and spend time with all desperately need deliverance from them too. This is a crucial point because it is reminding us that when we seek to share the gospel, we are not trying to sell something. So often, evangelism can feel like that. We can feel like we need to be a salesperson, trying to sell a product no one particularly wants. With that mindset, evangelism can feel very awkward, even embarrassing, and it can run the risk of becoming shallow. But if we remember that evil is evil, then that reminds us what the gospel is actually rescuing people from. It shows us how urgently the gospel is needed. And that shifts us away from thinking that we are selling something that people may or may not want, and instead it shows us that we are sharing something that people, without exception, desperately need.

This is where it is helpful to remember the difference between a car salesman and a car mechanic. When a car salesman sees a customer, usually they will need to use a lot of skill to convince the customer that the car in front of them is a good buy. So they need to be persuasive, they need to be confident, they need to be charming. And a huge amount rests on the talent of the salesperson, which is why I think it is a very hard and stressful job. A car mechanic doesn't need to bother with any of that. A mechanic doesn't have to charm the customer. A mechanic simply has to tell them what they need. And to get the customer on board, the only thing a mechanic needs to be is trustworthy. That is why, as long as the customer isn't stubborn or foolish, when a trustworthy mechanic tells them that they need something, they are going to listen.

In sharing your faith, you are much more like the mechanic than the salesman. We do not need to schmooze people into following Jesus as though our religion is the 'better buy' in comparison to all the others on offer. We need to remember that evil is evil, and the people around us desperately need us to accurately, humbly and sincerely tell them that the gospel is going to meet their deepest, most urgent needs. When someone is bruised and crushed by the reality of evil (and they might not even realise that that is happening), we are not coming to them with a bit of self-help therapy. We are coming to them with the only thing that will actually rescue and restore them.

This is where our motives have got to be right. If our motivation lies in a desire for people to listen to our religion and realise that we are right, then there is a real danger that the people we speak to may very well realise that our biggest concern is for ourselves. But if our motivation is that people would be rescued from evil and from all the devastation that it brings, then the people we speak to will see that our biggest concern is for them. The more we recognise that evil is evil, the more our motivation will arise from the urgent needs that are all around us. We must always remember that Jesus never said, 'I came to get a big flock of people following me.' Jesus said, 'I came to seek and to save the lost.'

Secondly, recognising that evil is evil reminds us of *why the gospel is utterly brilliant.* So yes, a clearer understanding of evil shows us how broken the world is and how precarious humanity's circumstances now are. But although that's crucial, recognising why the gospel is needed isn't enough. On its own, that truth can result in an evangelism that is simply proclaiming an alternative to bad news as though, in a world of evil, following Jesus is the least-rubbish option. But the gospel is far better than that! And we see that by recognising that evil is evil. That's because a clearer understanding of evil shows us just what Jesus is rescuing us from and just what an incredible difference Jesus can make to our lives. That difference manifests itself in wonderful ways:

In a world full of evil, Jesus gives us a better identity. No matter who you are or what your story is, in Jesus you are a precious, beloved, treasured child of God. That means you don't need to deceive your way into success; you don't need to use people to gain status; you don't need to chase satisfaction in a sinful pleasure, and you don't need to take revenge when you are hurt in order to feel better. You don't need any of that. In Jesus you are loved, valued, respected and gifted. He gives us an identity that fills the gap in our hearts that nothing else can fill. When we point people to Jesus, *that's* what we are offering them.

In a world of evil, Jesus gives us a better morality. Our culture today tells us that life is dog-eat-dog; Jesus tells us to bind up the wounds of the broken. Our culture encourages us to indulge ourselves; Jesus tells us to control ourselves. Our culture says that what we are in private is up to us; Jesus wants us to be pure right to the very depths of our heart. Our culture loves getting; Jesus tells us that giving is far better. Our culture delights in exposing people's mistakes; Jesus says do not judge. Our culture is quite willing to lie; Jesus cannot lie. Our culture has often masked abuse; Jesus will call every single injustice to account. Our culture is full of division, inequality and prejudice; Jesus calls everyone, no matter their gender, race, status or history, into a beautiful family of unity and equality. When we point people to Jesus, *that's* what we are offering them.

And in a world of evil, Jesus gives us a better destiny. The reality of evil has stained every generation of human history, and it casts a long and dark shadow over our future. This is probably why people don't like to think about what lies ahead. As individuals, the inevitability of death looms over all of us. For humanity as a whole, the threat of self-destruction is real, whether through war, disease, climate change, disaster, or a combination of them all. Either way, it feels like ultimately evil will win. Humanity seems destined for destruction. Jesus changes all of that. Jesus has come to break the power of death, Jesus has come to give us eternal life, and Jesus has come to restore the universe into a new heaven and a new earth where all the curse of evil will be gone forever. That's what Jesus has come to achieve. That's the new destiny that we can have in Him. Because of Jesus, evil will never win! That's what makes the gospel so utterly brilliant. When we point people to Jesus, *that's* what we are offering them.

Evil is most definitely a problem. Not because it undermines the existence of a good and powerful God, but because it is destroying both us and the world that God created for us to enjoy. But the

114

answer is not to ignore evil and never think about it. We have to acknowledge the reality of evil, we have to get a better grasp of the evilness of evil. In fact, humanity is the only part of creation that can really see that evil is evil. But not only that, as a human, you are the only creature capable of communicating the message that can actually deliver humanity from evil. When it comes to evangelism it is easy to feel like we can't do it. The truth is the opposite; we are the only ones who *can* do it.

So often, our evangelism is hampered by the mindset that thinks that the gospel isn't urgent and that the gospel isn't brilliant. Both of these are lies. The gospel is the most urgent thing that the people around you need to hear this week. The gospel is the most brilliant thing that the people around you will hear this week. We can share our faith because we have a message that is urgent and brilliant. To help us see that, we have got to remember that evil is evil.

STUDY QUESTIONS:

1. Looking at the culture around us, can you think of ways in which evil has become acceptable, entertaining and useful? Can you see ways in which it has happened in your own heart?

2. How has 'evil' been misunderstood in relation to Christianity? What does a biblical understanding of evil look like?

3. How can we abhor evil without looking judgemental, superior or self-righteous?

4. In what ways does an understanding of evil help us see the urgency of the gospel? How can this help us share our faith?

5. In what ways does an understanding of evil help us see how brilliant the gospel is? How can this help us share our faith?

6. How should the reality of evil shape our motives in evangelism?

Chapter Nine

People are People

◇◇◇

I once knew a man who lived a long way away from me who passed away several years ago. He was one of my favourite people. Full of fun, friendly, kind, enthusiastic, great company, a man who always lit up any room he went into. He was a wonderful person to be around. I also knew a man who lived in the same place who was a convicted criminal, had served several years in prison, a heavy drinker, reckless with money, a womaniser, probably a racist, definitely didn't care if he offended people. He was someone you knew you had to be careful around. What would have happened if the two of them met? Well, that would have been impossible, because they were both the same person.

You can probably think of lots of people that you could describe in the same kind of way. One of the biggest paradoxes that we will ever encounter is one that we come across multiple times every single day: People. People are an astonishing mixture of astonishing things. They can be the source of immense joy, they can be the source of awful pain. They can accomplish the most incredible things; they can do the most stupid things. They can be so beautiful; they can be so horrible. People are amazing, people are appalling; perhaps most of all, people are perplexing. But that's the way they are. People are people. And as we seek to share our faith, that is a reality that we must never forget.

Recognising this immediately guards us against two pitfalls that are very easy to fall into in evangelism. On the one hand, we must never think that people are projects that we can fix. That kind of mindset can lead to an unhealthy evangelism that is probably mechanical, possibly patronising, maybe even manipulative. On the other hand, we can think that people are write-offs that no one can fix. That doesn't lead to unhealthy evangelism; it leads to no evangelism! People are not projects. People are not writes-offs. People are people. But what exactly does that mean?

Understanding people

Biblical anthropology is a fascinating subject. This is the doctrine that gives us the answers we need when we try to make sense of the people we see around us and the person that we see in the mirror. In fact, you only to have to read three pages into the Bible to discover why the homeless drug addict on your street who has made so many terrible choices still needs and deserves help, why spending £250,000 pounds a year on a terminal cancer patient is worth every penny, why a child adored by her parents chooses to smoke even though she's been told a thousand times not to, why domestic abuse is both abundant and abhorrent, why getting as much money as possible is sickening and it is satisfying, it just depends on who's getting it. The Bible explains this because it tells us that humanity is incredibly special and it tells us that humanity is badly broken.

Central to the biblical teaching about humanity is the fact that we have been made in the image of God. This is really what makes humans, humans. Herman Bavinck, a Dutch theologian, makes a really helpful point when he says that when it comes to the image of God, '[Humanity] does not just bear but *is* the image of God.'[1] Nothing else in creation is God's image bearer, humanity has a

---

1. Herman Bavinck, *Reformed Dogmatics* (vol. 2), trans. John Vriend, ed. John Bolt (Grand Rapids: Baker Academic, 2004), 533.

position of unique privilege and responsibility. Humanity is special in a way that nothing else in creation is.

Over the centuries, theologians have observed that this image bearing can be thought of in terms of two elements. At a broad level, there is what is sometimes called **the *structural* aspect of bearing God's image**. Basically, this is to do with the nature and capabilities of humanity. These reflect the nature and capabilities of God. So humanity can think, communicate, relate to others, make decisions, discern right from wrong, carry responsibility, and appreciate beauty, all in a way that no other part of creation can. And these are the capabilities that make humanity different from animals, minerals and plants. In other words, it is God-like qualities that make humanity unique.

At a narrower level, there is what is known as **the *functional* element of image bearing**. This refers more to how humanity uses the capabilities given. Theologians have summarised this functioning under the headings knowledge, righteousness and holiness, which are taken from Colossians 3:10 and Ephesians 4:24.[2] So, all the structural capacities endowed by God on humanity are to be used to know Him (which in a biblical sense means being in an intimate relationship with Him); to be like Him, consistently conforming to God's righteous standards; and to be for Him, set apart as those devoted to our Creator with purpose and purity.

To put it all another way, thinking back to the olden days when phones weren't smart, imagine you have never seen the handset and dial combination plugged in to a wall and you asked, 'What is it?' The answer is, 'A phone.' And then if you asked, 'What does it do?' the answer is, 'It phones.' Now pretend you are a phone and imagine you're seeing a human for the first time. You ask: What is

---

2. **Colossians 3:9-10** Do not lie to one another, seeing that you have put off the old self with its practices and have put on the new self, which is being renewed in knowledge after the image of its creator. **Ephesians 4:24** ... and to put on the new self, created after the likeness of God in true righteousness and holiness.

it? The answer: The image of God. What does it do? It bears God's image. That, fundamentally, is what a human is.

That all might sound odd and a bit mystical, but it actually makes perfect sense of the way we all speak. When someone asks you, 'What do you do?', have you ever said, 'I find food, I avoid danger, I sleep and I reproduce.'? Of course you don't. But when you answer that question by saying, 'I am married to my husband, I work as a teacher and I love going to the theatre,' you have just described activities that nothing else in creation does. You have described things that only a God-like being can do. That's what makes humanity beautiful and amazing. That's what makes you and the people you know so special and precious.

But that is only half of the story of biblical anthropology. Genesis chapter 3 tells us that humanity has rebelled against God causing sin to intrude into our experience. This has had a pervasive effect on what we are. At a structural level, the core elements remain. In other words, sin hasn't turned us into a new lesser category of creature. We still have the capacity to think, relate, communicate, decide, admire. But these have now been damaged and distorted by sin. So our thinking is confused, our relationships are strained, our communication is hampered, our decisions are skewed, our admiration is misplaced. Consequently, the way we function has been spoiled. So instead of knowing God in an intimate relationship, we are alienated from Him and in a position of enmity. Instead of conforming to God's righteousness, we fall short and miss the mark as sinners. Instead of living for Him as a holy people, we are polluted with sin, living for idols. So if you imagine the phone again, it's now rusty, damaged and crackly. Is it still a phone? Yes. Can it perform its function properly? No, not unless it's fixed.

Humanity is in exactly the same situation. We are still God's image bearers, we still have the structural components in place, we are still unique and special. But they are now distorted and damaged by sin, and as a result our functioning becomes the very opposite of what God created us to do. Tragically, instead of using our God-given capabilities to reflect Him, we are using them to reject Him. That's what makes sin so awful; we sin as image bearers. A horse is not a sinner because it is not an image-of-God-bearer. But we are. And when we sin, we're taking the qualities and privileges that make us so special, and we're using them to spit in the face of the God who gave them all to us.

The result of all this is that humanity is still made in the image of God, but now we are badly distorted. That is why you can look at people around you and see wonderful things and awful things. And when you look at yourself you can see a person who is the handiwork of God and you can see a person who has been damaged by the destructive power of sin. This is why if you ask anyone, 'Deep down do you believe that you are special?' They will almost certainly say, 'Yes.' But if you ask them, 'Deep down do you believe that you are perfect?' For that question, provided the person has at least a fragment of self-awareness, the answer is definitely going to be, 'No.'

And I think all this can be proved if you imagine that you are standing in a busy city and you can hear the noise of sirens cutting through the air. I grew up on a rural island, so hearing sirens was rare, which is why today I still get excited to see a fire engine, ambulance or police car with the lights flashing and sirens blaring. (I also get excited when I see trains, combine harvesters and double decker buses, because we didn't have any of them either!) Most people are probably fed up of the noise of sirens. But have you ever wondered why it is that sirens ring out so much in our towns and cities? Why do we need sirens, and why are they used? For two reasons. It is because bad things happen in a world that has been broken by sin. And it is because the people caught up in whatever is going wrong are still incredibly valuable. An emergency is an emergency simply and only because people are very broken and people are very precious. That is the way people are. People are people.

Humanity: Beautiful and broken

This tension between beauty and brokenness is captured very powerfully in Psalm 139. In the middle section of the psalm, David speaks about how he is the handiwork of God. 'For you formed my inward parts; you knitted me together in my mother's womb. I praise you, for I am fearfully and wonderfully made. Wonderful are your works; my soul knows it very well' (Ps. 139:13-14). But just a few verses later, David pleads with God to 'slay the wicked' (v. 19). That language doesn't sit comfortably with us today, and in one sense it is right that is doesn't. Now that Jesus has been crucified and raised, the conflict between the Kingdom of God and the Kingdom of Evil has moved to a new level where the devil has been overcome and his grip over the world has been broken. That is why our battle is not against flesh and blood enemies in the way that it was for David in the Old Testament era. Still, to understand David's words, try to imagine a militia standing on your street wanting to kill every man, abduct every woman, burn every home and starve every child in your community. That gives you a picture of what it meant to have enemies in David's time.

The key point for us is that, in terms of humanity, the verses of this psalm dramatically portray the amazing beauty and tragic brokenness of humanity. The fearfully and wonderfully made person of verse 14 is a person. The bloodthirsty wicked people of verse 19 are people. At no point do these verses describe anything other than people.

The beauty-brokenness tension is also visible in James chapter 3. Without outstanding perception of human behaviour, James writes:

> For we all stumble in many ways. And if anyone does not stumble in what he says, he is a perfect man, able also to bridle his whole

body ... For every kind of beast and bird, of reptile and sea creature, can be tamed and has been tamed by mankind, but no human being can tame the tongue. It is a restless evil, full of deadly poison. With it we bless our Lord and Father, and with it we curse people who are made in the likeness of God. From the same mouth come blessing and cursing. My brothers, these things ought not to be so (James 3:2, 7-10).

Using the example of speech, James highlights the beauty of humanity: We are made in the image of God so with our mouths we have the incredible privilege of having both the ability and the opportunity to bless God. But the very same tongues can curse people, the image bearers that God Himself has made. The result is that we are beautiful, able to bless God. We are fragile; liable to stumble in many ways. We are complicated; even our tongues are impossible to control. We are exposed; we can so easily be hurt by others' words. And we are deadly; our speech can be the poison that causes huge damage to someone else. James captures this tension so poignantly when he says, 'My brothers, these things ought not to be so.'

All of this combines to build a biblical anthropology that is in constant tension. We can summarise humanity in the following four statements. These are just a selection, many more could be added (and I'll explain the dotted line in a moment!):

Beautiful but **Broken**
Fragile but **Harsh**
Precious but **Difficult**
Simple but **Complicated**

Humanity is like a broken vase. Made beautiful, now broken. Fragile, but now with edges that can wound others and can self-harm. Precious, but the bits are all over the place. Made for a simple and wonderful purpose, but the task of putting everything right is huge.

Reaching out to those who are beautiful and broken

All our experience as people is shaped by this beauty-brokenness tension. Often, though, it feels like the brokenness bit of it is dominant. If you look at the news headlines, they're going to contain much more brokenness than beauty. And the fact that we put so much time and effort into looking and feeling more beautiful shows that feeling broken comes a lot more easily to us all. But the amazing truth of the gospel is that in God's eyes you've not stopped being beautiful. And because of that, He will not leave you broken. He has sent Jesus His Son to come and do a magnificent work of restoration. But most amazingly of all, for people like us to be fixed, Jesus had to be crushed. And in willingly doing so, Jesus has come to take broken humanity and make us His beautiful bride. All He asks of us, is to trust Him.

That's the message of the gospel. Our job is to share that message with the people around us. As we've been saying all along, that's a job that every one of us finds daunting and, because of that, we conclude that we can't do it. But you can. You absolutely can. And one of the key reasons why you can is because the people you are going to share it with are people. And if we remember that, it will help us overcome our fear and hesitation to talk about Jesus. But for that to happen, we have to remember that people are people, and that means that we have to remember what is written on both sides of the dotted line.

That's what Jesus did; He recognised the beauty-brokenness tension in humanity. That is seen so magnificently in the words of Mark 3:1-5:

> Again he entered the synagogue, and a man was there with a withered hand. And they watched Jesus, to see whether he would heal him on the Sabbath, so that they might accuse him. And he said to the man with the withered hand, 'Come here.' And he said to them, 'Is it lawful on the Sabbath to do good or to do harm, to save life or to kill?' But they were silent. And he looked around

at them with anger, grieved at their hardness of heart, and said to the man, 'Stretch out your hand.' He stretched it out, and his hand was restored.

Here Jesus saw the brokenness of humanity, both in the suffering of the man and in the cruelty of the crowd. But He also saw the beauty and preciousness of humanity. He is grieved because of the brokenness; He graciously heals because of the preciousness. His anger arises because, when it comes to people, this is not how things should be at all. At every step of His mission, Jesus knew that people are people.

We need to think the way Jesus thought. In other words, when we look at people around us, we need to look at both sides of the dotted line. So if you look on the right, it is telling you that the people around you are broken, harsh, difficult and complicated. You might think, well if that's true then I am never evangelising! But please think about it a bit more. That right side is telling you two absolutely crucial things. First, it's telling you straight away that you can't fix everything. That's why people can never be projects, the situation is way more complicated than that. That's why evangelism is only ever possible in the strength and power of the God who is God. You don't need to put every piece back together, you don't need to answer every question, you don't even need to find out if the person actually becomes a believer. And that's not discouraging; it is liberating! We just try and say what we can; God has to do the rest. But the right-hand side is also telling you something else. It is telling you that the people around you *need* your evangelism. To Jesus, brokenness, harshness, difficultness, and complexity do not repel Him. They draw Him. That reminds us that down that right side, you are not reading a list of reasons to stay quiet. You are reading a list of compelling reasons to take a deep breath, to take a step of faith and speak.

But if we look only at the right-hand side, that step seems cripplingly scary. That's why you also need to remember what is written on the left. The broken-harsh-difficult-complicated people all around you are also beautiful; they are the craftsmanship of God Himself, which is why they are never, ever to be written off. They are fragile; vulnerable and exposed to so many dangers. They are precious; more valuable than they have ever dared imagine. And they are simple; they are actually just another one of the things that you are. They are people. Made by God, made for God.

All of that means the structures are already in place for them to be ready to hear the good news of God's work of restoration. This is crucial to remember: the gospel is not a misfit message that needs to be rammed into people because it's incompatible with who they are. It is completely compatible with who they are. It is actually the most compatible truth that they can ever hear! It is the renovation programme that our damaged humanity desperately needs. That doesn't mean that people will instantly accept what we say. But it does mean that when you point someone to Jesus, you are simply pointing them to the place where they belong more than anywhere else.

Both sides of that line are crucial. The right hand tells you that it's not easy and you can't fix it all. The left hand tells you that trying to speak to your friends and family about Jesus is so, so worth it.

Reaching out as those who are beautiful and broken

But there's one final thing. People are people, so that includes you as well. When you look at the diagram, you are looking at a description of yourself. That means that **as you share the gospel, you need to be ready to acknowledge that you are broken.** You need to guard against any tendencies you may have to be harsh. You need to expect that not everything will be perfect and difficulties might arise along the way. You need to remember that you are complicated too, so please don't panic if you discover that you are carrying a whole web of strengths and weaknesses into any conversations you have.

But you must also remember that you are beautiful. You really are. You are beautiful in God's eyes. You are made with wonderful qualities. And even though the battle against sin continues, God the Holy Spirit lives within you and He is transforming you. You will probably feel like your words are messy and muddled, but every sentence that passes your lips is carrying the most beautiful message that humanity has ever heard. In a world that is so full of brutal cursing, your trembling voice is passing on the very words of eternal life.

You must remember that you are fragile. That means that sharing your faith might leave you feeling exhausted. It may leave you feeling guilty when half an hour later you remember all the things you wish you'd said. It might leave you feeling very worried, longing for your friend to come to faith, scared that all you've done is put them off. The moments when you share your faith may well be the times when you feel at your most fragile. But never forget that fragile jars of clay are exactly where God has placed the treasure of His gospel (2 Cor. 4:7).

You must remember that you are precious. You are God the Father's child, you are Christ's ambassador, you are the Holy Spirit's home. You might feel like your words are rubbish. But as the Father holds you securely, as Jesus stands alongside you, as the Holy Spirit guides you, and as heaven watches on, your words and actions are priceless.

And, last of all, you must remember that you are simple. That is not an insult; it is a relief! It's a relief because it means you don't need to become a superhero. You don't need to become a genius. You don't need to become an evangelistic machine. You just need to be you. The beautiful-fragile-precious-simple person that God has made you to be. You love Jesus. You need Jesus. You long for others to know Jesus too. They are just people, like you. People are people. All they need is a simple, ordinary, not-particularly-impressive disciple to talk to them. They need a person just like them, which means they need a person just like you.

STUDY QUESTIONS:

1. Can you think of examples of how you have seen the beauty of humanity and the brokenness of humanity this week?

2. With reference to our mouths, which can bless God and curse the person made in the image of God, James writes that 'these things ought not to be so'. Can you think of other ways in which this is true in regard to people? What difference can the gospel make to these situations?

3. In what ways has sin affected the structural and functional aspects of our image bearing?

4. What do you admire about how Jesus understood the people with whom He interacted?

5. In evangelism, why is it important to remember that people (including you) are broken, harsh, difficult and complicated?

6. Likewise, when sharing our faith, why is it important to remember that people (including you) are beautiful, fragile, precious and simple?

CHAPTER TEN

A Church Family is a Church Family

One of my (many) weaknesses in life is fizzy juice. I absolutely love a cold can of fizzy juice from the fridge; it is just marvellous! Among my favourites is Dr Pepper, but for many years it wasn't, for the simple reason that I had never tried it. The reason I didn't try it was because I didn't like the sound of fizzy juice that tasted like pepper. Turns out Dr Pepper doesn't taste of pepper at all; it is fruity and sweet and very tasty. When I first tried it, I was pleasantly surprised at how nice it was. The marketing team at Dr Pepper have long since realised that there are many people like me, who don't like Dr Pepper because they have never tried it, so for years Dr Pepper has been advertised as the drink that has been 'so misunderstood'. I definitely misunderstood it. I didn't try it because I thought it would taste of pepper. I didn't think for a minute that it would be sweet.

The only thing more misunderstood than Dr Pepper is the church. For many people, following Jesus and coming to church appears less like drinking a lovely sweet can of juice and much more like eating a stick of celery; it is probably good for you, it is something that you really should do, but for most people it is highly likely to be pretty unpleasant.

Joking aside (and with apologies to all celery lovers), one of the biggest challenges we face in terms of evangelism is the fact that, long before they ever come close enough to taste and see that God is good, people jump to the conclusion that being a Christian is not going to be particularly sweet. No doubt there are many reasons for this, but behind them all lies one massive misunderstanding: People think that following Jesus and being part of a church is going to feel like a form of slavery.

There are two sides to this problem. One is that our sinful nature leaves us in a state of rebellion against God. So, just as Adam and Eve wanted to be their own masters, so do we. We don't want to have to obey God, we don't want anything interfering with our routines, we don't want to be held to account for our failings. Consequently, you hear people say what has to be the most monumental misunderstanding in all of history: 'I don't want to follow Jesus because I will lose my freedom.' There's no doubt that for people on the outside, Christianity is often seen as slavery.

The other side of the problem is that Christians have actually made Christianity look like slavery. Throughout the history of the church, and still today, there have been frequent occasions when Christians have been harsh and cruel towards others. We have also defined our lives as disciples in terms of everything that we are not allowed to do and in terms of making sure that we tick all the right boxes expected of us. The result is that not only has Christianity been misjudged by those who stand without, it has been misrepresented by those who stand within.

All of this is a massive problem. It stifles discipleship and robs us of assurance and confidence because it leaves us thinking that God is an angry taskmaster whom we have to impress. And it cripples our evangelism because it makes following Jesus, and being part of His church, look painful and joyless. And what makes it so tragic is that it is all based on a monumental misunderstanding of the gospel. Christianity is *not* about slavery. Christianity is about *family*. Now, that is not some nicey-nicey optimism to make Christianity sound appealing. It is a cast iron truth of dogmatic theology. For every part of our Christian lives, and especially for our evangelism, it is crucial that we never forget that the Church family is a *Church family*.

To see this, we need to think about some of the big categories into which theology is divided. These big categories can easily sound complicated and it might be a lot to take in, especially when you are so close to the end of this book! But it's really worthwhile to learn more about these. So, even though we are near the end, let's roll up our sleeves, let's take one final deep breath, and let's dive in.

The study of theology is divided up into various subject areas. For example, **Biblical Theology** looks at how God has progressively revealed Himself through the Bible, from Genesis right through to Revelation. **Systematic Theology** organises the truths revealed in the Bible so that we can summarise and understand everything that the Bible has got to say about a particular topic – like God, or sin, or the atonement. **Practical Theology** explores how these truths are to be applied in the life and experience of the Church. So, biblical theology follows the history of God's revelation from the beginning of the Bible to the end, systematic theology identifies key topics and summarises everything the Bible teaches about each one, and practical theology shows us how to take what we've learned and apply it to life today as members of a local church and as missionaries in a field that is ready for harvest. In all three of these theological subjects, family is crucial.

Family and biblical theology
From the very beginning of the Bible, family is at the heart of God's purposes. Adam and Eve are united in marriage and instructed to raise children. That union of a man and a woman is essential for the growth and survival of the human race; it is also a source of immense joy as people share in the beautiful family bonds of love between husbands and wives, children and parents. These bonds, however, have been badly damaged by sin. There

is now hostility and cruelty between men and women, there is neglect and resentment between children and parents. All of that is a consequence of humanity's rebellion against our Creator.

But the study of biblical theology reveals God's plan of salvation, and at the heart of it is family. In Genesis 3:15, God promises salvation through the woman's offspring. In Genesis 12, God promises to make Abraham into a great family through whom all the families of the earth will be blessed. And the rest of the Old Testament is the story all about a family.

This is something that is easy to miss. When we think of Israel in the Old Testament, we can often instinctively think primarily in terms of a nation, probably because Israel today is a nation like all the others. And yes, Israel was a nation in the Old Testament too. But first and foremost, Israel was a family. The name Israel comes from the name that God gave to Jacob in Genesis 32. Israel the 'nation' is actually just Jacob's descendants or, as the Bible frequently says, 'the children of Israel'. That means that, when we read about the Israelites in the Old Testament, we must think in terms of family before we think in terms of nation.

In the north of Scotland (where I am from) most people have a surname beginning with Mac. 'Mac' is the Gaelic word for 'son', so to have a Mac-something surname means that you are a descendant of a particular person: MacDonald, MacLeod, MacArthur, MacRae and so on. When it comes to Old Testament Israel, it is perhaps helpful to think of them as the MacIsraels. They were a family, all descending from Israel (Jacob). Their identity, their administration, sometimes even their jobs, were all structured around their family relations.

The MacIsraels, however, were a broken family. In the early part of the Old Testament they were slaves in Egypt for centuries. But although God freed them from slavery and brought them into the Promised Land, they quickly turned away from Him. They argued, divided and even at times went to war with each other. By the end of the Old Testament, there was only a remnant of the MacIsraels left.

However, the prophets that God raised up among the MacIsraels gave amazing promises that God had not forgotten this family.

That brings us to the New Testament, and the family theme continues. In fact, the very first thing you read in the New Testament is a family tree (Matt. 1). Jesus has come as the Messiah that the MacIsraels were longing for. He is a MacIsrael Himself, but He has not come just to restore the MacIsraels of the Old Testament. He has come to make a new MacIsrael family. He has come to fulfil the promise given to Abraham that all the families of the earth will be blessed. That is why, when Jesus came into the world, John tells us that 'to all who did receive him, who believed in his name, he gave the right to become *children* of God' (John 1:12). That is why Paul tells us that 'it is those of faith who are the *sons of Abraham*' (Gal. 3:7). Jesus came to call all nations into God's family. Biblical theology is the story of a family.

Family and systematic theology
Family is also crucial to systematic theology. The two pillars of family are marriage and parenting. These correspond to two of the most glorious doctrines of systematics: **Union with Christ and the doctrine of adoption.** Let's unpack each of these a little.

The theology of how we are saved is called soteriology (from the Greek 'soteria' which means salvation and the Greek 'logia' which means something along the lines of 'studying something cool'!). And at the very core of Christian soteriology is union with Christ. That is how someone is saved, by being united to Jesus Christ by faith. We are united with Him in His death (see Rom. 6:1-11). That means that, when He died, He took all our sins upon Himself as our substitute. We are also united to Him in His resurrection (see Rom. 6:1-11 again!). That means that, just as death has no power over Jesus and instead He lives forever, so too the power that sin and death had over us has been broken, and we can receive resurrection life because we are united to our resurrected Saviour. The whole of our salvation is grounded on the fact that we are united to Jesus, or as the New Testament repeatedly says, we are 'in Christ'.

And that union is described in terms of marriage. Jesus came as the bridegroom (Mark 2:19). We are joined to Him as a wife is joined to her husband (Eph. 5:31-32). And the great climax of God's plan of salvation is the marriage supper of the Lamb (Rev. 19:9 and 21:2). We are united to Jesus: we are His bride; He is our Bridegroom. Marriage points us to what God wants to do with us through His Son. In fact, the whole reason humans have marriage instead of simply mating is to point us to the ultimate marriage; the union of Christ and His Church.

But alongside that, if we are united to God the Son, that means that we can enjoy the same liberties and privileges that He enjoys. That means that, just as He knows God as His Father, so too can we. Or as John told us, we have the right to be called the children of God. Soteriology follows a beautiful order: by God's grace, He chose not to abandon us. Instead, He calls us; He opens our eyes like a new-born and we are given a new heart. That means that we can see both our sin and our Saviour and we come in repentance and faith; by that faith we are justified so that our sin is not held against us. Instead, the Judge whom we had wronged so much doesn't simply acquit us; He adopts us and takes us into His family as His beloved children, transforming us to become more like His Son, our elder brother, Jesus Christ. And that's what makes the gospel so amazing: the God whom we rejected has never given up on us and His goal is not just that we would bow at His feet as worshippers; His goal is that we would fall into His arms as His beloved children.

That work of adoption involves the whole Trinity: The magnificent words of Ephesians chapter 1 tell us that God the Father plans and wants it, God the Son pours out His own blood to accomplish it, God the Holy Spirit comes into our hearts to guarantee it. God's great purpose in salvation is to bring us into His family.

And the key point is that that family salvation is *not* slavery. Paul makes that so clear in Romans 8:

> For you did not receive the spirit of slavery to fall back into fear, but you have received the Spirit of adoption as sons, by whom we cry, 'Abba! Father!' (Rom. 8:15).

He says the same thing in Galatians 4:

> And because you are sons, God has sent the Spirit of his Son into our hearts, crying, 'Abba! Father!' So you are no longer a slave, but a son, and if a son, then an heir through God (Gal. 4:6-7).

But the place where this is made clearest of all is when Jesus told the Parable of the Lost Son (Luke 15). After rejecting his father and ruining his life, the son realised the mess he was in and returned home hoping that maybe, just maybe, he would be allowed to be a slave in his father's household. But as he returned, his father ran to him, clothed him and put a ring on his finger, and in doing so he made absolutely clear that that broken boy was never, ever going to be a slave. He was a son.

This is why the Bible can talk about our salvation as redemption. Redemption means to be bought out of slavery. That's what Jesus has come to do. He is our Redeemer. He redeems us from slavery to sin by laying down His own life as a ransom. He has come to set us free. He has come to bring us into His amazing family.

Family and Practical Theology

So, family runs right through biblical theology: it is at the core of systematic theology, but **it is also absolutely essential for practical theology.** Practical theology takes in a whole range of topics: pastoral care, leadership, what a church service should look like, church discipline and more. All of these must be understood in terms of family, not slavery.

The pastoral care of the church is care for a family. The people who come to church are neither customers nor staff; they are family. That is why loving one another is so crucial in the life of the church. It is not a bonus if we love one another; it is the acid test of whether or not we actually love God (1 John 4:20).

Leadership in the church is the leadership of a family. We are not taskmasters, we are not bosses, and we are not managers. We must lead the church with the same care and wisdom as we lead our own families. That's why one of the qualifications for eldership is to be able to look after your family, because that is exactly what being an elder is all about (1 Tim. 3:4-5).

When we meet together for worship, we meet as a family. That's why, if there is more warmth and joy at home after the church service than there is during the service, there is something far wrong. The sacraments tie into this: Baptism welcomes new members into the family; the Lord's Supper is a meal shared by the family for the nourishment of the family.

And, perhaps most importantly of all, **church discipline is all about family.** The church has got this desperately wrong many times. So often, when a Christian falls into sin, churches have concluded that the best way to protect the church family is to push the person out. But that never protects the family, because the person you are pushing out *is* family. A Christian who makes a massive mistake is not a slave who needs to be sacked. They are a child who needs to be healed. That's why the goal of church discipline is always restoration. That's why, if you ever have to deal with someone who has fallen into sin, you must always ask the question, 'What would I do if this were my own child?'

Christianity is not about slavery. It is about family. 'When the fullness of time had come, God sent forth his Son, born of woman, born under the law, to redeem those who were under the law, so that we might receive adoption as sons' (Gal. 4:4-5).

Family and sharing your faith

All of this is crucial as we seek to share our faith. That is because the battle between slavery and family doesn't just surface in biblical, systematic and practical theology. It also spills over into our minds as we struggle to step out and share our faith with the people around us. And consequently, we can be crippled by feelings of slavery as we try to evangelise.

This can happen in two ways. On the one hand, we can feel that we are going out as slaves. So, there's a sense of pressure: we need to evangelise as Christians. There's a sense of guilt: you are failing as a Christian if you don't do it. There is a sense of fear: we're probably going to do it badly, but you better make sure you do it. Going out to share the gospel can easily feel like slavery.

But on the other hand, we can also be held back by the feeling that when we try to share the gospel, we are going to sound like we are calling people into slavery. In other words, if we feel like slaves, then calling people to be like us means calling them to feel like slaves as well. That is not a particularly appealing message to share. And we fall into this trap because we get caught in a cycle that sees Christianity as slavery, therefore, we act like we are slaves, and therefore we make it look like slavery. And so the whole depressing cycle goes on and on.

That kind of thinking is crazy. It is also heresy. Christianity is *not* about slavery. And thinking that it is gives a woefully inaccurate picture of what we are doing when we share our faith. This is because an understanding of evangelism based on slavery tends to think in the following terms:

Intimidation: You've got to share your faith because God will be angry if you don't. Likewise, the people you are talking to have got to come to church because God will be angry if they don't.

Coercion: If you don't share your faith, there will be serious consequences for you and even more so for the person you need to talk to.

Criticism: You've been failing at evangelism, so you need to up your game. And the people who aren't coming to church have got to sort themselves out too.

Restriction: You've got to tell people to stop all the wrong things that they are doing in their lives, but make sure that you don't get too close in the process.

Fear: They need to be saved. You need to evangelise. You are going to be in trouble if you don't.

Intimidation, coercion, criticism, restriction and fear. A family built on those kind of things is not a family. It's a prison.

And this is why we have got to remember that the church family that God the Father loves, that Jesus died to establish, and that God the Holy Spirit is sanctifying is a church *family*. And **a family is not built on intimidation; it is built on friendship.** When we go out with the gospel we do that as friends together, supporting one another, encouraging one another and praying for one another. It is not a competition as to who can get the most converts. It is not a contest as to who can be the best evangelist. We do it as friends who are all part of the same family. And we are calling people into a community of warm, kind, welcoming gospel friendship.

A family is not built on coercion; it is built on compassion. As we go out with the gospel we are all feeling the same feelings; we are nervous but excited, shy but hopeful, inadequate but still longing for God to be at work. And the people we meet don't need our condemnation. They need our compassion. They're getting hammered enough by life as it is; we are not going to add more blows. We are coming to them to offer healing and hope, just like Jesus did.

A family is not built on criticism; it is built on joy and celebration. As we go out with the gospel, we are looking forward to the amazing moment when we will see lives transformed by Jesus. And as heaven rejoices over a sinner who repents, we will be joining in.

A family isn't built on restriction; it is built on protection. As we try to share the good news, we are in this task together. That means supporting and helping each other, and never leaving each other to do it all alone. We evangelise as a team. And for the people we are trying to reach, our message is not a message of dull restriction that is going to squeeze every last drop of fun out of their lives. We are not pointing them into a cage. We are offering them an open door to the freedom of knowing Jesus, the freedom of being able to thrive as we follow Him instead of being ground down by trying to impress everyone around us, the freedom of knowing that death has lost its sting, and the freedom of knowing that you are safe and secure in God's family together.

And maybe most importantly of all, **a family is not built on fear. It is built on love.** As you seek to share the gospel, you are doing that as a child of God who is so utterly and wonderfully loved. Every step you take, every text message you send, every invitation you offer, every conversation you try to have, at every single moment God is looking at you and saying, 'I love you. I have loved you forever and I will love you forever. You are my precious child. Don't be afraid.' But at the same time, when God brings you to someone with whom you are sharing your faith, God is also saying, 'I love them as well, and I want them as part of our family too. Please tell them that.'

As you share the gospel, you are going out from a family and you are calling people back into that family. It is God's family. A family of friendship, compassion, celebration, protection and love. It is not slavery. It is a family. That is why, if God uses you to help someone come to faith in Jesus, the end result is not that you've got the task done. The end result is that you now have a brand new brother or sister. How awesome is that?!

This is where everything we've been trying to say comes together. God is God. It is only in complete dependence on Him that we can share the gospel; it is only through Him that any harvest will come. You are you. You have relationships, contacts, friendships that place you in a unique position to be used by God where you are and as you are. And those people that God has placed around you are people. They are so precious, and they need Jesus so much. The God who is God has a wonderful goal. He wants all of these – Him, you and them – together in His amazing, beautiful, wonderful family. The more we understand theology, the more we realise how incredible God is and the more we see how brilliant His plans are, then we will stop saying to ourselves, 'It's too hard; I can't share the gospel.' Instead, we will find ourselves saying, 'It's too good; I can't keep this to myself anymore.'

STUDY QUESTIONS:

1. In what ways do you think Christianity has been made to look like slavery?

2. In what ways can sharing our faith sometimes feel like slavery?

3. In your community, do you think biological family bonds are stronger than church family bonds? If so, why do you think this is the case?

4. In what ways can you see the emphasis on family running through the big story of Scripture? Why is this emphasis important for evangelism?

5. Compare 'Intimidation, coercion, criticism, restriction and fear' with 'friendship, compassion, celebration, protection and love'. How can we guard against the former and cultivate the latter?

6. As we reach out to the community around us, how can we be better prepared to welcome people into the church family?

Postscript:
God is not You and You are not God

∞∞∞

God is God and you are you. No matter who you are or what your strengths and weaknesses might be, God is big enough, wise enough, kind enough and powerful enough to use you to share the good news of Jesus with others. That makes every day of your life so exciting. Just imagine what the God who is God can do with the person who is you! But before we finish, there are two final things to remember.

The first is that *God is not you.* That means that there are lots of things that God will (or won't) do that might not be what we want or expect. So, for example, God's timing might not be your timing. That means that opportunities for sharing our faith might not always be at convenient moments; they may happen when we least expect; they may happen when we really don't feel ready. It also means that things might take a lot longer than we would like. Often, we want to see someone go from unbelief to faith in Jesus in a few minutes or hours, at the very most a few days. But what if it takes years? Is it still worth it? Of course it is.

God's methods might not be your methods either. We might expect a conversion to come through a great conversation, a powerful sermon, or a study group for seekers. These are all brilliant. But God might also use a text message, a song, or a combination of a thousand things. And He might even use people that we don't agree with. That's really important to remember. There are two things that I am firmly convinced of: one is that I believe wholeheartedly in Reformed theology. The other is that I believe wholeheartedly that God is constantly using Christians who don't agree with me in order to bring new converts to faith in Jesus. God will often surprise you, but that is because He is not you, He is God.

The second point to remember is that *you are not God*. That means that you are not, and never will be, the cornerstone on which someone else's conversion stands. That cornerstone is only ever Jesus Christ. And that is so incredibly reassuring because it means that you never have to do everything. You don't have to have all the answers; you don't have to be the beginning, middle and end of someone's journey to faith; you don't have to do everything perfectly. In other words, when it comes to sharing your faith, you can do a rubbish job, and amazing things can still happen because you are not God. He is God. You are you, so just focus on being you, and let God carry on being God.

You are not God; God is not you. The truth is the other way round. God is God and you are you. And together, the God who is God and the you who is you can spread the good news of Jesus Christ today, tomorrow and for the rest of your life. You really can do it. And amazing things really can happen.

Bibliography

Bavinck, Herman. *Reformed Dogmatics*, vol. 2, translated by John Vriend, edited by John Bolt. Grand Rapids: Baker Academic, 2004.

Chapman, John. *Know and Tell the Gospel*. Second edition. New Malden: The Good Book Company, 1998.

Pippert, Rebecca Manley. *Out of the Saltshaker and into the World*. Revised edition. Nottingham: IVP, 1999.

Tice, Rico. *Honest Evangelism*. Epsom: The Good Book Company, 2015.

Christian Focus Publications

Our mission statement –

STAYING FAITHFUL

In dependence upon God we seek to impact the world through literature faithful to His infallible Word, the Bible. Our aim is to ensure that the Lord Jesus Christ is presented as the only hope to obtain forgiveness of sin, live a useful life and look forward to heaven with Him.

Our books are published in four imprints:

CHRISTIAN FOCUS

Popular works including biographies, commentaries, basic doctrine and Christian living.

CHRISTIAN HERITAGE

Books representing some of the best material from the rich heritage of the church.

MENTOR

Books written at a level suitable for Bible College and seminary students, pastors, and other serious readers. The imprint includes commentaries, doctrinal studies, examination of current issues and church history.

CF4•K

Children's books for quality Bible teaching and for all age groups: Sunday school curriculum, puzzle and activity books; personal and family devotional titles, biographies and inspirational stories – because you are never too young to know Jesus!

Christian Focus Publications Ltd,
Geanies House, Fearn, Ross-shire,
IV20 1TW, Scotland, United Kingdom.
www.christianfocus.com